"Chris Jarvis has created a unique approach to solving business and life challenges by taking inspiration from the wilds of Africa. His analogies reveal some hard-won and deeply insightful truths that will help just about anyone better understand the impediments that are stopping them. His advice on overcoming both self-created and external obstacles are priceless and his style and voice make for fun, totally painless reading. Well worth your time."

RON PENNA
Founder of Quest Nutrition and Legendary Foods. RonPenna.com

"I love Chris' brilliant intellect, wonderful sense of humor, and no-BS approach to business and life. Chris is first and foremost a teacher who wants to help people by eliminating the unnecessary stress and aggravation around money. His motives are pure, and his advice is invaluable."

JACK CANFIELD
World's #1 Success Coach.
Founder of the billion-dollar Chicken Soup for the Soul® publishing empire.

"With decades of entrepreneurial experience and investments in more than eighty startups, I've learned this fundamental truth: To build a company of significance, one must have the elevated vision and perspective of a giraffe. Chris Jarvis is the embodiment of this, a forward-thinker whose uncanny insight into what lies ahead is truly exceptional. As I embark on what is the most ambitious venture of my career with Fundify, I'm thrilled to have Chris at our side."

JOSH CHODNIEWICZ
Co-founder, Art.com/Allposters.com. Founder, Fundify.com

"Chris has one of the most innovative minds I've ever encountered. His creativity combined with his in-depth knowledge of accounting, tax, law, and insurance is a unique blend of skill sets that produces amazingly productive solutions and opens your eyes to business opportunities you may never have imagined. Everything Chris writes is worth reading ... more than once!"

GORDON LOGAN
Founder and Chairman of SportClips.
International Franchise Association Entrepreneur of the Year
and Hall of Fame Award Recipient

"Over the past twenty-five years, I have seen Chris innovate in multiple industries and motivate people from diverse backgrounds and experiences. His unusual combination of technical ability and emotional intelligence allow him to simplify very complicated situations so problems can be overcome quickly and easily."

MOHANJIT JOLLY
Founding Partner, Iron Pillar. Former Partner, DFJ and Garage Technology Ventures

"What sets *Be the Giraffe* apart is its ability to bridge personal growth and business acumen. In a market flooded with personal development and business guides, *Be the Giraffe* stands out as a beacon of simplicity and clarity."

DAVID MELTZER
Co-founder, Sports 1 Marketing. Former CEO Leigh Steinberg Sports & Entertainment

"When it comes to life, relationships, and leadership, we can learn a lot from the giraffe. This book will stretch you!"

MORAG BARRETT
Founder of SkyeTeam.com. Bestselling author of *Cultivate, and You, Me, We*

"The Venture Café community found your big-picture thinking and practices both inspiring and useful. You're a real giraffe and welcome here anytime."

SHAWN HAKIMI
Director, Venture Café Cambridge

"After my first meeting with Chris, I knew he had a remarkable gift. He has a knack for decoding complexities into simplified concepts that solve big issues. Full of personality and fresh new perspectives. Chris addresses many important matters that come with success and gives advice that even the most successful entrepreneurs need to hear."

REBECCA FINELL
Founder of Boon, Finell Co, and Zip Top

"Rapid technological changes will shape the landscape of finance and banking over the next decade. Smaller companies that embrace the idea of leaving the herd and doing things differently, like the giraffe does, can take market share from much larger firms that are slow to adapt. *Be the Giraffe* is a must read for all of our managers and leaders."

SHANA DE PAOLI
CEO UBank

"I've known, and worked closely with, Chris Jarvis for over fifteen years. What most people recognize about Chris are his creative financial and business skills (both of which are truly unique). But his most unique gifts are his genuine concern for others and his willingness and ability to help solve problems. Chris has helped me to look at my firm and my career from different perspectives. He was an invaluable resource helping me prepare my company for an eight-figure exit. I recommend Chris without reservation to any business or business owner looking for an ally who can make a meaningful impact."

DAN ACETI
35-year financial services executive

"An enormously gifted speaker and writer, Chris is the ultimate teacher's teacher. He's exceptionally creative, insightful, articulate, wise and passionate. His purpose-driven approach simply sees problems differently and, accordingly, solves them with an elegant simplicity. When I'm struggling with how to think through a challenge or communicate a topic, he's the one I call. I'm profoundly grateful to call him my friend."

CHRIS ERBLICH, ESQ.
Partner, Husch, Blackwell, LLP. Chairman, TFO Phoenix

"If you want to grow—really grow—personally and in your business leadership, learn from this book. The giraffe will surprise you."

BRUCE CARDENAS
Entrepreneur and business coach. BruceCardenas.com

"The best presentation I have heard in forty-three years! His expertise as a business consultant and financial advisor gives him a unique perspective that make his training meetings valuable, memorable and forward-focused."

TOM ARCHER
CEO, Elite Marketing Group. Former Chairman, Insurance Designers of America

"Having guided up to Everest and Machu Picchu and down the Amazon, *Be the Giraffe* is a great way to unleash nature's power and send your life and your business in the direction you want."

DENNIS "MR. SEDONA" ANDRES
CEO, Sedona Private Guides

"For years, I wanted to leave corporate life, start my own thing, and make my dream life a reality. I kept finding excuses and avoiding my potential—until I started working with Chris. He not only encouraged me to believe in myself, but he also showed me what to do to remove real and imagined obstacles. Chris helped me navigate the complexities of my employer, my family, and my own ego. When I used his advice in new business conversations, I was able to secure $16,000 of revenue in my first month alone. There is no looking back! If you are done with mediocrity and ready to live into your potential, talk to Chris Jarvis."

HANNA HERMANSON
Founder, Dream Life is Real Life. Forbes Coaches Council Member

"As someone who has built several multimillion dollar companies from less-than-scratch, struggling with all the necessary steps along the way, Chris hits the nail on the (lofty) head in *Be The Giraffe*. His perspectives are fun, fresh, helpful, and memorable. A must-read for anyone struggling to find their purpose and wanting to achieve more in business and in life."

BRYCE JENKINS
Founder of The Virtuous Collective. Author of *11 Unpopular Reasons Why I'm Rich* and *You're Not: Stories and Lessons from My Unlikely Success*

"Our team has worked on over 500 brands—and none fits better than the giraffe. Jarvis has the uncanny ability to help you and your entire team see past the noise and see a better path to reach ambitious goals. Multiple times, we have hired Chris to help us address major challenges. Let *Be the Giraffe* be the catalyst that will get you, your company, your team and your objectives all in alignment and positioned for success!"

RAMON PERALTA
Founder, Peralta Design. Author, Launch Your Brand

"As a TEDx organizer, I have worked with hundreds of successful speakers. Unsurprisingly, 'Mr. Giraffe' Chris Jarvis stands out among them all—and not because his talk went viral. The value of his advice and his genuine concern have helped me professionally and personally. He's the real deal—walking the walk and talking the talk. I'm honored to call him a friend."

GARY DOHERTY
Derry Londonderry TEDx Organizer. International PR Expert

"Where do I start? Chris has helped me, my team, and my clients on numerous occasions. He asks seemingly benign questions that lead to much deeper discovery. A true teacher, Jarvis has a way of guiding you to a creative solution without telling you what to do. *Be the Giraffe* is an eye-opening, thought-provoking book that will help you navigate your biggest challenges—in business and in life."

BRETT D. SCOTT
Founder & CEO, Super-Charged Freedom

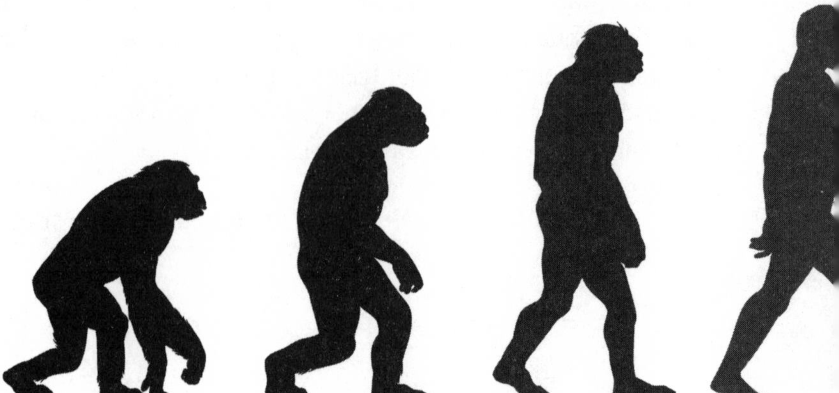

CHRIS JARVIS

14 Paths to Reach Higher in
Business and Life

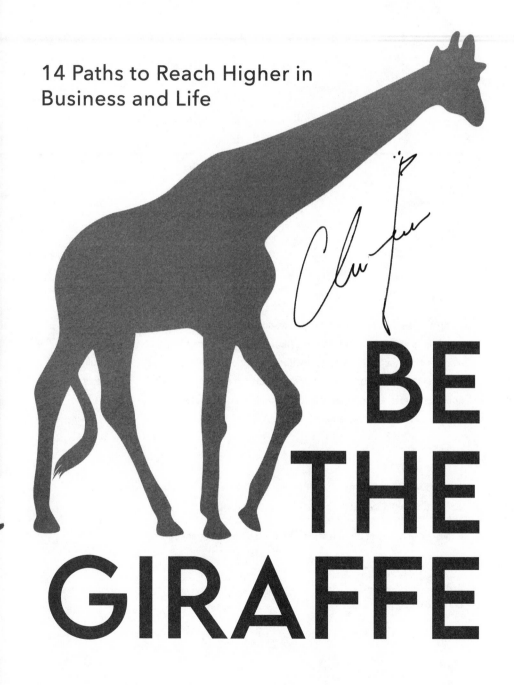

BE
THE
GIRAFFE

Fedd Books
P.O. Box 341973
Austin, TX 78734
www.thefeddagency.com

Published in association with The Fedd Agency, Inc., a literary agency.

ISBN: 978-1-957616-91-9
eISBN: 978-1-957616-61-2
LCCN: 2024901914

Printed in the United States of America

To my mom Dot Fogarty, your enormous heart is what
allows this giraffe to see better paths for myself and
others. Thank you. I love you.

Chrissy

Elevate your perspective

See a better path

Be the Giraffe! :)

CONTENTS

ABOUT THE AUTHOR

Chris Jarvis has thirty years of experience helping millionaire entrepreneurs and billionaire families build and preserve wealth.

Authoring seventeen books, appearing on Bloomberg Television, and being quoted in *The Wall Street Journal* gave Chris exposure to many wealthy and influential people. Along the way, he discovered the unusual paths to standing out and reaching the highest levels of success. After applying these lessons to build and sell his own firm, he learned that he must do things differently if he wanted to be happy and healthy. The giraffe would lead him to stick his neck out to see things differently.

"After making millions of dollars and helping others do the same, I lost my younger sister and business partner unexpectedly, saw both parents diagnosed with incurable cancer, and spent four years and $700,000 in legal fees chasing down the money owed to me from the sale of my company. I pretended that things were OK, but they weren't. I was stressed out, overweight, and my body was starting to reject me. When I tore my Achilles and hurt my back enough to require spine surgery, the signs were too much to ignore. There had to be a better way.

My story of overwhelm must not be too uncommon—the 2022 TEDx Talk "Surviving Ain't Thriving" was the second most watched of the year and has been viewed by 4.5 million people.

I now help executives, entrepreneurs, and affluent families manage the complexities and interconnectedness of their money, their businesses, and their personal lives.

I proudly sit on the dean's advisory council for the University of South Carolina School of Medicine, working toward delivering quality healthcare to underserved areas and underrepresented populations. I am also on the board of the prestigious IC^2 Institute at the University of Texas-Austin, exploring economic development solutions for rural communities."

LEARN MORE

https://chrisjarvis.me/about-chris/

FREE BONUS

I wrote *Be the Giraffe* to elevate perspectives and reveal paths to different outcomes.

To help you Money Differently, Business Differently, and Life Differently, I have included additional resources absolutely free!

Here is what you will receive:

- Video training, explaining how to get the most out of *Be the Giraffe*
- Exercises and worksheets
- Assessment tools for you, your family, your colleagues, and your employees
- E-newsletter subscription
- Useful links
- And much more!

You get everything at www.chrisjarvis.me/btg/bonus
or by scanning the QR Code below

www.chrisjarvis.me/btg/bonus

FOREWORD

BY DAVID MELTZER

As you embark on this exciting journey with Chris Jarvis' new book *Be the Giraffe*, you might be wondering why I, David Meltzer, am writing this foreword. Perhaps the idea of me being compared to a giraffe has left you intrigued, or maybe even a bit perplexed. Rest assured. This is just the beginning of the surprises awaiting you in these pages.

My introduction to Chris Jarvis came on the recommendation of a long-time client and friend Brett Scott. What struck me about Chris was his willingness to drive an hour for what was meant to be a brief five -minute meeting at one of my events. Predictably, our conversation extended well beyond the planned time and, soon after, Chris became a guest on my livestreamed show "Office Hours."

To my surprise, Chris and I discovered that our paths, though unconventional, shared similarities. Who would have imagined that a mathematician and recovering actuary would leave behind a lucrative career solving financial puzzles for the wealthy just as a lawyer, dealmaker, or sports agent would transition into the realm of motivational speaking? Life has a way of leading us down unexpected paths, doesn't it?

In my journey, encapsulated in my book *Connected to Goodness*, I've experienced the highs and lows that come with financial success. Like the evolutionary process, my personal growth involved significant shifts, often unnoticed by those closest to me. In the pursuit of wealth, I almost lost what mattered most: my family and friends. The market crash in 2008 brought about my own "Big Bang" resulting in the loss of a vast fortune and a subsequent bankruptcy.

Adapting to these challenges enabled me to find a new direction, one centered on purpose, family, and a more meaningful life. Chris, too, has faced his share of adversity, including being kicked out of a very profitable company that he started, a divorce, the loss of his younger sister, and the tragedy of having both parents diagnosed with incurable cancer. His unsurprising emotional and physical health complications led him to search for purpose. Our paths converged through shared experiences of transformation and resilience.

In *Be the Giraffe*, Chris brilliantly explores the unique qualities of the giraffe and translates them into life lessons. The giraffe's extended neck, symbolizing an elevated perspective, allows it to see beyond the horizon, paving the way for paths untraveled. Similarly, my own journey toward a better life began with vulnerability—a willingness to acknowledge my mistakes and take responsibility for the impact they had on others. Shedding the masks of success and embracing my imperfections transformed me into someone relatable and authentic.

What sets *Be the Giraffe* apart is its ability to bridge personal growth and business acumen. Chris delves into fourteen distinct giraffe qualities and demonstrates how they can be applied to enhance various aspects of your life, from health and finances to career and relationships. Each chapter not only imparts valuable life lessons but also offers practical business applications. For someone like me, whose aspiration revolves around making money and helping others, the integration of these lessons into professional interactions is invaluable.

In a market flooded with personal development books and business guides, *Be the Giraffe* stands out as a beacon of simplicity and clarity. Chris combines a brilliantly simple metaphor with practical applications that can be implemented immediately. This book is not just a guide; it's a transformative experience waiting to unfold.

So, buckle up and prepare for a journey that will not only inspire you but also equip you with the tools to thrive personally and professionally. As you read these pages, may you find the courage to stick your neck out, embrace your vulnerabilities, and reach new heights—just like the remarkable giraffe.

INTRODUCTION

ARE YOU READY TO REACH HIGHER IN LIFE AND BUSINESS?

HOLY CRAP, I AM A GENIUS.
(OH MY GOD, I'M A TOTAL FRAUD.)

Happy Friday to me. After twenty-five years of (literally) breaking my back, I sold my company, Jade Risk. No, the previous sentence was not hyperbole. Within six weeks of the closing, I was scheduled for the spine surgery I had been delaying—mostly because I was too busy running my business.

Even though the surgery was scheduled, along with ten to twelve weeks of painful recovery, I hadn't planned to slow down. Despite new ownership, I would retain a key position in the business. Millions of dollars were already wired into our accounts—plus, I had millions of dollars of deferred payments and millions more in incentives from my sale. Did I finally plan a long vacation? Take the time I needed for my health? Nope. I doubled down and launched a new consulting firm to create multiple income sources—that was my plan, anyway.

> LIFE GIVES US SUBTLE HINTS.
>
> WHEN WE DON'T TAKE THEM SERIOUSLY, THEY BECOME FAR LESS SUBTLE.
>
> —CHRIS JARVIS
> *LEARNED THROUGH DECADES OF IGNORING*

That weekend, I received a call from my sister Jennifer. Dad had discovered our sister Dee unconscious in her apartment. He called 911 while desperately giving his own daughter CPR. The paramedics transported Dee to Our Lady of Fatima Hospital in North Providence, Rhode Island—a quarter-mile from our childhood home. The five of us were together when we learned Dee would not survive her accident. She was a week shy of her forty-fifth birthday.

Spine surgery gives you a lot of time in bed alone with your thoughts. The death of someone close to you can stir up and amplify feelings. With too many thoughts flying around my head, feelings pouring out of my heart, and opioids flowing through my veins, I felt the calling and a sense of obligation to help people who struggle to help themselves (like Dee). I didn't know exactly what that looked like, but the universe seemed to like that idea too; eight weeks after Dee's passing, I was fired!

When the buyers of my company failed to hold up their end of the deal, counsel advised me to:

1. File a multimillion-dollar lawsuit, which I later won on all counts.

2. Prove I did nothing wrong by continuing to honor the noncompete I signed.
3. Because of #2, walk away from my clients and industry and do something else.

From feeling like I was on top of the business world to being fired from a company I built was quite a drop. The sudden loss of my sister was a deep shock, and the pending lawsuit was surreal and painful. Weirdly, one of the most positive experiences I had in those four months was spine surgery.

From a combination of legal necessity, moral obligation, and grieving, I redirected my efforts toward helping others.

When I learned that Jack Canfield, co-creator of *Chicken Soup for the Soul* and other successful endeavors, was writing *Mastering the Art of Success*, I took a flier and submitted a chapter for consideration to be included in the book. My contribution, "Increasing Sales without Ever Selling," was not only accepted, but it also was recognized as "outstanding contribution" from the publisher. Do you know what was even cooler? I was invited to be interviewed on Jack's video channel.

Why not? I had some free time. If I want to change lives, I thought I should probably meet the guy who sold billions of books and was in *The Secret*, a movie about the power of the Law of Attraction. Maybe I'll figure out what makes him unique and get a few pointers on changing lives from someone who has touched so many.

In January 2018, when I got onto the set at the Roosevelt Hotel, the video production went as expected. Microphone, check, check, check. Lighting. Bring out makeup. Let's get extra powder on that bald head to eliminate the glare. Then, "Action!" Jack was very comfortable on camera and gave me a big smile that lasted throughout his warmup questions. Then, he threw me a curveball.

"What advice would you give your younger self?"

What?! I was not expecting that question. I paused for what seemed like an eternity until these words came out of my mouth:

"I would tell myself not to waste so much time trying to fit in. You're different. You're not going to fit in, and everything will be okay. In fact, things will be way better than okay if you just be yourself and not worry about what others want you to do or who they want you to be."

In the first of many accidental discoveries, the giraffe was born.

WHY THE GIRAFFE?

I could use the obvious metaphors of standing tall or rising above the rest. That would be an easy layup, especially for the tallest kid on the savanna. No. There's more to the giraffe and more for you.

How the giraffe became so tall is a more interesting conversation about evolution. The *Be the Giraffe* trademark may have given you a hint.

To achieve the great height they are known for, the giraffe has evolved to grow long legs and an even longer (relatively speaking) neck than any other animal. Here is your chance to play scientist. Ask yourself: Why did the giraffe evolve this way? And, what advantages did the giraffe achieve by evolving in this way?

The giraffe's long neck allows it to see things other land animals cannot, giving the giraffe a unique and elevated perspective. At upwards of eighteen feet in height, the giraffe reaches leaves that other animals can only dream of tasting. Up there, in that rare air, the giraffe has no competition whatsoever.

In your life, what kind of trouble could you have avoided if you knew something dangerous was heading your way? Better yet, what kind of success could you have enjoyed if you could have seen what was ahead—well before those around you?

If you knew what was coming, good or bad, and had little to no competition between you and others for what you wanted, how much easier, more efficient, and more enjoyable might your life be?

This is why we want to be giraffes. We want to elevate our perspective to see better paths in our lives and to avoid danger. When we are willing to elevate and change what we see, we can evolve in how we think and what we do. This is my goal, my wish, and my prayer for you on your quest to *Be the Giraffe*!

WHO NEEDS *BE THE GIRAFFE*?

Initially, I began to write this book for my younger self, the one with fewer than thirty candles on his birthday cake, more than his fair share of hair on his head, and no idea how many lessons he was about to learn—the hard way. I envisioned well-worn copies of *Be the Giraffe* on the desk or nightstand of every first-time entrepreneur or ambitious visionary.

In nature, evolutionary change may take thousands, if not millions, of years to be discovered. It only took me five years and fourteen chapters to see what *Be the Giraffe* is about and who will get the most out of it.

Along this path, I realized that *Be the Giraffe* is not a book for a younger me. This message is for everyday me—especially today!

If you're at all like I am, perhaps you've felt underappreciated, uninspired, and unhealthy for more than a few stretches in your career. Maybe you feel disconnected or distracted. Are you overworked, overextended, or overcooked?

You shouldn't feel embarrassed or ashamed that you are in this predicament; you're in good company. Although, as we'll discover soon enough, you're actually in bad company.

DIFFERENT IS BETTER THAN BETTER

There are many ways to improve your personal and business lives or to uncomplicate your life as a business owner who may or may not be able to tell where personal ends and business begins. A partial list of all the things I have tried throughout my life and career includes individual and group therapy, life and executive coaching, print and audiobooks, transformational workshops, subscription-based online communities, mastermind groups, and peer groups like Young Presidents' Organization (YPO) and Vistage.

Each endeavor has its inherent benefits and its drawbacks. On top of that, the effectiveness of any experience is impacted by timing, your mindset, and the skill of the person trying to help you. It's an inexact science, but I have done a lot of research. After countless hours and hundreds of thousands of dollars, I wanted *Be the Giraffe* to have multiple mechanisms and media to include the best elements of many techniques. I also wanted the *Be the Giraffe* materials to do some things these other approaches don't do well, or at all.

Be the Giraffe is different in three ways:

1. Context, not just content. Personalized for you, based on your behaviors.
2. Comprehensive. Combines business, finance, and transformational experience.
3. Colorful and memorable. Everything is supported with colorful animal metaphors that are fun and easy to remember.

In the next chapter, I will invite you to take the Find Your Wild Factor Assessment. Usually $19.95, the link and code in this book allow you to access this unique tool for FREE! You will receive a personalized nineteen-page report providing invaluable context as you continue through *Be the Giraffe*.

I created this tool to help you measure five areas of your life. In understanding your natural strengths and biggest challenges, you can decide where to focus your efforts throughout this book. With this context, you will be able to apply all the lessons from *Be the Giraffe* to your individual situation.

Be the Giraffe is a personal development guide that will help you look at the three areas of money, business, and life differently and collectively. You do not have to be a shark and devour everyone in your path to become successful and wealthy. Contrary to the self-proclaimed enlightened life coaches you may find in your Instagram Reels, you don't have to sacrifice financial rewards to be happy. *Be the Giraffe* will help you look at and improve all three areas.

In the research for two of my books, *6 Secrets to Leveraging Success* and *Giraffe MONEY*, I studied the award-winning economic research of Dr. Emmanuel Saez and shared stories from my millionaire and billionaire clients. One of the most valuable takeaways in both books was that super-successful people are very comfortable being different.

This is where mindset comes into play and brings the third leg of the stool into the program, making *Be the Giraffe* unique. After selling my company, I trained and worked with Jack Canfield, who gave me incredible insights into the power of the mind and the ability of people to overcome great challenges.

We could audition animal spokesmodels for "different" all day long, but I'd still pick the giraffe. Stay with me, and I bet you'll agree.

The giraffe shows us a better path to improving our finances, health, career, and relationships—and having more fun with all of it.

I'M A TOTAL FRAUD.

Okay, back to my moment in the video interview.

"Things will be way better than okay if you just be yourself and not worry about what other people want you to do or who they want you to be."

When I heard those words come out of my mouth, I must confess that I was quite impressed. Look out Jack Canfield and Tony Robbins, Jarvis is ready for his close-up!

Then, for reasons I can't explain, a second perspective became clear.

I've spent most of my first fifty years trying to fit in. As a result, I was avoiding, ignoring, or neglecting the true, different, authentic me.

I wasn't convinced everything would be okay. I was scared, caught like a zebra in the headlights between the status quo and the life I wanted to live.

Fraud. I wasn't being true to myself or the higher aspirations I was somehow blessed to hold.

I needed to take action. I needed a teacher, a really weird mentor. Yoda wasn't available, but I spotted an even better one. And that, as the poem goes, has made all the difference.

So, this book is for the younger me, the five-years-ago me, and the today me. And I believe it's for you.

Being the giraffe is not about increasing your income, the value of your business, or advancing your career. It may do any, all, or none of those things. Being the giraffe is about helping you find and enjoy everything you want in life—and more than you ever knew you wanted.

The next fourteen chapters will not focus on the height and majesty of the giraffe; that would make the book predictable and uninteresting—the same way you would be unsurprised to learn that someone 6'10" plays basketball. Instead, we will focus on the weaknesses and vulnerabilities of the world's tallest mammal. In understanding how the giraffe has evolved and adapted to become more vulnerable, you will learn invaluable lessons to help you persevere, stand out, and reach much greater heights in life and business.

CHAPTER 1

GET OUT
OF THE WEEDS

*TO FIND OUT WHAT'S AHEAD OF YOU,
WOULD YOU ASK A ZEBRA OR A GIRAFFE?*

What can giraffes teach us about ourselves and our businesses?

Many herbivores, including giraffes, spend nearly every waking moment eating and drinking. I guess I'm a grazer, but that's another story.

Though giraffes are herbivores, they are very different from the other plant-eating mammals. While antelope, zebra, buffalo, and wildebeest (also called "gnu") primarily eat grasses, the giraffe eats tree leaves. The nutritional value of grass and leaves is similar, so the difference isn't in what the giraffe eats. The significance is where the giraffe eats.

As you might imagine, this difference also affects the taste. Would you like something fresh off the tree or a salad tossed by wildebeest's filthy hooves?

Herbivores are primarily grazers who spend most of their lives with their heads buried in the weeds or at shoulder height amidst a herd of countless other animals. They have little to no idea what is happening on the outskirts of the herd, let alone what is lurking beyond the trees or bushes. Grazers, like zebras and wildebeests, rely on the groupthink movements of the herd to tell them where to go for their next meal. Their survival depends on it. But giraffes are different.

"I'd like a table for one—with a view!" The giraffe eats standing up, preferably to bite the fresh leaves of the acacia tree. While chewing, the giraffe's head is well above the plains, bushes, and any predators in the area. With an unimpeded view in all directions, the giraffe can survey, stroll, and munch all day—without hurrying after the herd.

The giraffe is gloriously independent.

FOR YOU

Each chapter will begin with a unique characteristic of the giraffe—similar to the one you just read. In each chapter, the phrase FOR YOU is your cue that the pages that follow will show how to apply the chapter's giraffe lesson to stand out in your personal life. This may be a way to improve your physical or emotional health, develop a better mindset, strengthen or repair relationships, or simply have more fun.

You've likely heard the phrase "stuck in the weeds." It means you are so busy doing that you don't have time to think about what you're doing, why you are doing it, how you could be doing it better, or what you could be doing instead. I am not a historical linguist, so I can't give you the phrase's origin, but it sure sounds like the life of a grazing herd animal to me. Are you stuck in the weeds?

- Does your routine feel predictable and repetitive and repetitive?
- Is your schedule full of tasks other people ask of you?
- Are you great under pressure because you have had so much practice?

If you're like I was for most of my career, you may have an overwhelming email inbox and an endless to-do list. I was so overcommitted at work and home that I didn't have time to think about a better life, let alone the time and energy to explore ways to change my life.

When living in the weeds, there's always just one more clump of grass to eat before we're "finished"—or until the next blades appear under our nose. Ironically, the more goal-oriented and competitive we are, the more we focus on achieving little goals and the more likely we are to ignore the more important ones. When our strong survival instincts kick in, our sense of purpose devolves into simply making it through the week.

Feel a little lost? You're not alone. Only 25 percent of Americans report having a clear sense of purpose.

If you're like I was for much of my adult life, you may find yourself alternating between mindlessly working and desperately searching for purpose or passion with the occasional pursuit of pleasure. When you don't know what you truly want to do, where you want to do it, or who you want to do it for, it's natural to look at what other people are doing. Looking to others for guidance in a digital world where millions of people are seemingly in the palm of your hand can lead to even greater anxiety with a Fear of Missing Out (FOMO).

> **Are you wondering what emails, texts, DMs, or snaps may have arrived as you read this page? Let's do something else instead.**

If only 25 percent of Americans report having a clear sense of purpose in their life, what does that mean for the rest of the population? An optimistic view would be to accept the philosophy that "ignorance is bliss." If you believe that "I don't know what I don't know" and "What I don't know can't hurt me," you might conclude that most people are happy.

The antidote to ignorance is education—and numbers don't lie. People with household incomes over $75,000 are most likely to experience FOMO. The top 30 percent of earners in this country are worried about what other people might be doing.

According to *Psychology Today*, approximately 30 percent of millennials always or very often feel lonely. Approximately 72 million millennials (born between 1981 and 1994) represent 22 percent of the US population.

These statistics reinforce the idea that too many of us are going through life on autopilot.

This chapter aims to help you change the way you look at your life, become aware of what you need to do more of, and learn how and why you have been sacrificing these important parts of your life. All of these are important to help you find a better path to a life that excites you, brings you joy, and gives you the best opportunity to be happy, healthy, and impactful.

LEARN THE GIRAFFE THREE-STEP

Step one to getting out of the weeds and onto a path that maximizes what you get from this book is understanding where you are. Step two will be to craft the vision of where you want to go. Step three will be how you plan to make the changes necessary to reach your goals.

STEP 1
WHERE AM I NOW?

STEP 2
WHERE DO I WANT TO GO?

STEP 3
FIND A BETTER PATH

GIRAFFES ARE INCLUSIVE, NOT INVASIVE

According to the National Wildlife Federation, "An invasive species can be any kind of living organism … that is not native to an ecosystem and causes harm. They can harm the environment, the economy, or even human health."[1]

How could an invasive species hurt us? Invasive species may negatively affect native species due to direct interactions like predation and competition. For example, invasive species may … outcompete native species for resources such as food, light, prey, and habitat.[2]

Giraffes are not invasive, they are inclusive. *Be the Giraffe* is not about getting everyone to act, think, or be the same. On the contrary, this book is about identifying, embracing, and leveraging the qualities that make each of us different. The giraffe is the only animal to evolve to become more vulnerable and, somehow, it always seems to find a way to turn challenges into opportunities and weaknesses into strengths.

To *be the giraffe* means taking an elevated perspective as we look at both our positive and negative tendencies. This is neither to be boastful nor to be critical. We elevate so we can identify the best path to being ourselves and getting the most out of who we are.

A few years ago, I noticed that people were increasingly worried about "getting canceled." Subsequently, the need to find a tribe became paramount and a great deal of our shared quest for individuality has been lost.

I wanted to do something to try to help draw attention to the situation. First, I recorded a TEDx Talk, "Surviving Ain't Thriving—Break Free From the Herd." Apparently, the message hit home, as it was the second most popular talk of 2022, with over 4.5 million views at the time of this writing. If you feel like you are constantly putting out fires, chasing your tail, or jumping from one emergency to the next, you might enjoy this TEDx Talk.[3]

Second, I spent fourteen months creating the Find Your Wild Factor Assessment to help people look at their lives differently. If you are like I am, you may have taken a handful, or over a dozen, personality tests in the past. You read in the opening chapter that my advice to a younger self was to stop trying to fit in with some elusive group. I took this advice and created a short, fun, memorable assessment that is different from any quiz or assessment you've ever taken. In four minutes, your answers to simple, multiple-choice questions will score your life in the areas of:

1. Health
2. Finances
3. Career (or Purpose)
4. Relationships
5. Fun

After answering twenty multiple-choice questions, you'll immediately receive a personalized nineteen-page report and meet some animal guides to help you on your journey.

Take your free Find Your Wild Factor Assessment now at www.findyourwildfactor.com. Use coupon code 17CJ44 to save yourself the $19.99 price.

Think of this as a "choose your own adventure" story, and you're the main character!

FOR BUSINESS

In each chapter, you will find a unique giraffe lesson and then tips for applying it to your personal life to help you reach higher. After this personal application, you will see the words FOR BUSINESS. This is where you will find tips for applying that chapter's giraffe lesson to your business or workplace. Whether you are the owner, a manager, or a dedicated employee, these lessons will help you to see things differently so you can have greater impact and success.

Being in the weeds is also known as working in your business versus working on your business. And the same applies to your career.

So many professionals are so busy doing what they do that they never take the time to figure out how to do it better, faster, cheaper, more efficiently, or more enjoyably. Is enjoyment even allowed?

According to a statistic I just made up, 100 percent of business owners hate their business at least twice per month. This sometimes coincides with payday, but other factors come into play.

Being a giraffe means you see differently and think differently. Giraffes constantly survey, assess, and plan so they can find a better path before it's too late.

When I was running Jade Risk, a firm I founded to help business owners create and run their own insurance companies, I built solid relationships with my thirty-six corporate clients. I was helping them manage risks, lower expenses, and leverage capital. These relationships generated millions in recurring revenues and a seven-figure annual profit. As I set out to capture highly profitable relationships that clients couldn't dream of leaving, I built a business that held me captive.

I had structured the business such that I, Chris Jarvis, was integral to nearly every client. I had no time to do anything creative or innovative because I was too busy weed-eating.

If I had taken an hour to lift my head and look around, I could have made decisions for the betterment of myself and my clients. But that's the simple step we overlook because it's so ... simple. Yeah, I really mean it. I'm asking you to take an hour to do nothing but look around. Look in the mirror, look at your loved ones, look at your career.

I failed at strategic planning for the same reason that most people do: I was too busy. Because I had so much to do and never enough time to get it done, I looked at strategy as just another thing to add to my endless list.

When I finally dedicated time to strategic planning, I found the only way out was to sell the company to a strategic buyer. Within fifteen months of that session, we closed on a sale that freed me from the operational and administrative hell and returned my investors their principal plus $1.1 million in profit.

Maybe that's worth an hour of your time.

WHAT'S UP, DOC?

After working with thousands of doctors and lawyers over the last twenty-five years, I found that most of them resisted doing long-range strategic planning. Why? Because the time they would have to spend working with consultants was time they could be doing another procedure or billing another client for their work. They felt they couldn't afford to take time out of their billable work to strategize.

Dr. Larry was an exception. In his early forties, he and his wife Sasha retired from the Army and moved to East Texas to begin a private practice as a Mohs surgeon, a subspecialty of dermatology. By the end of his first week, he was booked solid for months! Despite the crazy hours with patients, Larry took time to study the unusual business of medicine.

Larry built multiple ancillary income sources in an ambulatory surgery center and dermatopathology lab. He implemented systems for patients and staff that allowed the practice to see more patients and make more money, attracting more dermatologists.

I was with Dr. Larry when a private equity firm from Boston came down for a tour of his practice. We dropped them off at the hotel, and Larry asked, "What do you think?"

I replied, "If they want a cheap practice to buy, it won't be yours. If they are looking for a flagship practice to use to grow a huge multi-state dermatology hub, you'll have an offer within the week."

A very attractive offer was made within days. Within a few years, this practice acquired the services of hundreds of doctors, was sold multiple times to different private equity firms, and became the most extensive dermatology practice in the United States.

TAKE YOUR BUSINESS "ON SAFARI"

Little did I know, this book started writing itself when I was a kid watching countless nature shows with my dad. In 2003, I had the once-in-a-lifetime opportunity to go to southern Africa on a four-week photo safari with my dad and my dear friend Lee Kaplan. Whether we were in a Land Rover, boat, canoe, or on foot, we needed to always be alert. There was very little doing and a great deal of observing—which led to an amazing amount of learning.

Getting out of the weeds in business means to stop doing and start observing. Your vision will expand, your perspective will gain clarity, and you'll be able to see threats and opportunities.

TODAY'S REACH

At the end of each chapter, you will see this image of the giraffe sticking its neck way, way out. Notice it's looking and reaching well outside the box. This short section will give you something to think about during your day. Right now, chew on this.

Giraffes eat leaves, not grasses. This seemingly small difference between the giraffe and every other herbivore on the savanna makes a monumental difference.

Literally and figuratively, the other grazing animals spend most of their lives with their heads in the weeds, unaware of what is going on more than a few feet away. Other than the precious few at the front of the herd, these animals have no idea where they are going next and no say in the matter.

Being a giraffe starts with getting your head out of the weeds so you can see where you are. As we begin this journey, I've created two tools to help you:

1. Find Your Wild Factor Assessment: As I mentioned earlier, you have free access to this assessment, and your personalized report will help you see the weeds and rise above them. Use Code 17CJ44 when you visit www.findyourwildfactor.com.

2. Elevate Your Business Assessment: This tool will help you look at your business in five areas: strategy, sales and marketing, operations and management, financial stability, leadership, and personnel. If you are considering selling your company and want a buiness assessment you may complete the Elevate assessment at https://giraffeu.typeform.com/Elevate.

Take your time as you go through these exercises. All answers are correct. Most importantly, be kind to yourself as you review the results. The purpose of these assessments is to give you a better idea of where you are right now. This will help you figure out where you might want to go—and how best to get there.

I promise there's a method to this madness, and the message is not to "Try harder" or "Set big gorilla goals!"

You're going to *Be the Giraffe*, and you're gonna like it.

CHAPTER 2
AVOID THE MASSES
AND THE ASSES

SMART ANIMALS FOLLOW THE FOOD.
NOT-SO-SMART ANIMALS ARE THE FOOD.

—CHRIS JARVIS
LEARNED THROUGH WATCHING
COUNTLESS NATURE DOCUMENTARIES

In the last chapter, I told you that some of my fondest and most impactful childhood memories were with my father, learning about nature
together—starting with *Mutual of Omaha's Wild Kingdom* and culminating
with a month together in Africa.

If you happen to share the same interest, perhaps you can imagine
the episode highlighting the great African migration. Here's the British bi-
ologist with the unmistakable voice:

"Today, we meet the untold thousands of zebras, giraffes, and wildebeest who have migrated thousands of miles across the Masai Mara.

These weary travelers must now face the imposing and treacherous Mara River. There is no easy place to cross. The raging water is up to ten feet deep in the middle.

"Millions of animals approach the unstable riverbanks with caution—for good reason. Hidden in the muddy waters are living dinosaurs. Nile crocodiles, as long as eighteen feet and over 3,000 pounds, have been looking forward to this day for months.

"As the herds crowd the river's edge, anticipation and drama build. Survival instincts win out as they take the plunge. Most make it. Many don't. The scene is gruesome, especially as stately giraffes are toppled in the grip of one, then several, toothy death rolls."

Cue the *Lion King* soundtrack, and a slow-motion montage begins.

Remember those scenes?

It's a trick question. The answer is yes—and no! Everything about this annual event described above is true, except no herd of giraffes was decimated by crocodiles. Why? Because it has never happened.

AVOIDING THE MASSES

There are many reasons why this gory scene does not include the tall namesakes of this book. First, giraffes are nonterritorial, nonmigratory animals. They are free to roam wherever they desire. Giraffes may congregate in groups of up to a half dozen. These groups, called "towers," do not have a formal hierarchy and do not form large herds.

They enjoy a freedom of movement that other animals do not, nor are they impacted by the weather due to the deep roots of their food source. Contrast that to the zebra, buffalo, or wildebeest that form large herds and migrate following the rains.

I lived in Boston, Los Angeles, and Austin before settling in the Dallas suburbs. I know something about traffic and the time we waste in it. I'll avoid further comparisons and simply point out that giraffes avoid traffic and traffic jams altogether.

Herd animals stay in large groups to be safe. They rely on safety-in-numbers, but this strategy is a double-edged sword. Sure, a group of predators will only take down one member of the herd at a time. Since there might be thousands, if not hundreds of thousands, of fellow commuters on the plains, you may like your odds. Do you remember the famous words of Lloyd Christmas in *Dumb and Dumber*? When asking Lauren Holly's character about the odds of them getting together, she replied, "One in a million."

His response: "So you're telling me there's a chance!"[4]

This may seem crazy, and though the movie is ridiculously clever and silly at the same time, it is also profound. There is safety in numbers for a herd until your number is up. And I haven't seen any PBS specials about water buffaloes dying of old age, have you?

Another drawback is that predators can easily find herds of hundreds, thousands, or even millions of animals. When a single animal leaves the "safety" of the group, it is immediately targeted by the many stalkers who patiently follow the herds. For that reason, once you are in, you can never really get out "safely."

Giraffes don't need to have the protection of a herd. They avoid the buffet by going places other animals are not. When they stumble across predators, it is usually an accidental encounter, and giraffes are surprisingly well-equipped to handle their foes, even in that scenario.

FOR YOU

Since human beings are also mammals, like those that form the constant great migration of animals in Africa, let's look at the four reasons animals form herds:

1. Protection from predators
2. Improved feeding opportunities
3. Social interaction and communication
4. Reproduction advantages

The factor that has the greatest impact on humans is the third—social interaction and communication. With language and technology, humans can communicate with nearly every other person on the planet to navigate the other three areas. In the previous chapter, we learned that three-quarters of Americans do not feel they've found their life's purpose. It makes sense that "highly evolved humans" would utilize the communication and technological tools that they developed to see what others are doing.

Unfortunately, this pendulum swings both ways, and not all communication is positive or helpful.

Consider this herd mentality I witnessed up close:

In 2020, the COVID pandemic turned political and people's fears led to many rational and irrational arguments; some of the most heated debates centered around education. Administrators were unprepared and confused. Teachers were put into impossible situations. Parents were afraid to send their kids to school and afraid they might kill those kids if they didn't go back to school.

My wife Heather was uniquely qualified to help. As a national board-certified English teacher with nearly twenty years of experience, she completed her master's in education virtually in 2009. Then, starting in 2011, she taught virtual high school. She was a decade ahead of everyone and could identify with all three groups—the teachers, administrators, and parents.

In September 2020, after meeting with multiple committees, Heather crafted the letter below and pasted it into both the conservative and liberal Facebook groups people in our town had created.

> In August 2020, I met with our local school district to give some guidance on creating a dedicated virtual school to be used during the 2020–2021 school year. This plan also discussed how virtual education should be integrated into face-to-face (f2f) learning to support students who were absent from school for a lengthy period of time. Despite my expertise in this area, these ideas were largely ignored.
>
> As we all move forward with the beginning of a new school year, hold your school boards and districts accountable. Demand high-quality education for your student(s) regardless of the delivery method. This is our

time to develop innovative educational experiences and delivery methods.

Do not be quiet. Educators and districts are in uncharted waters; DO NOT assume they are on the right track. Ask questions and hold those in administration answerable for their ideas and plans.

Please remember this: Teachers are being asked to do the impossible. We must advocate for them and our students. Let us challenge the people in charge to make innovative change, but let us do it with kindness and compassion, recognizing that mistakes will be made along the way.

Heather Jarvis, M.Ed

The result? The post was taken down, and Heather was kicked out of both groups.

One of her friends even messaged her, "I can't tell what side you're on." Side? She was on the side of the students—this should not be political!

When you are lost among the masses, all you can see are the asses around you. From this story, you can see that there is also the danger of the masses becoming asses when they get nervous and feel threatened. Groupthink can be a dangerous, significantly limiting, and very frustrating thing for anyone—especially a giraffe!

SUCCESS—AND THE LACK OF IT—IS IN YOUR HEAD

In my book *6 Secrets to Leveraging Success*, there is a segment, "You Have to Be Psychotic to Be Successful." This refers to having a non-herd mindset. The good news is that, unlike how much money your parents had, how much education you have, or where you grew up, you control your mindset. It doesn't matter whether you were born rich or poor, male or female, black or white, gay or straight, Democrat or Republican, devoutly religious or atheist. No matter where you may have started, where you have been, or where you are heading, you and only you get to control the way you think.

The good news is that the pendulum does swing, and you can change your mindset. This is of the utmost importance because, if you want to be the giraffe, you absolutely and positively have no other choice but to change the way you think. Elevating your perspective is the only way to find a better path to get more out of your life. Let's see how the most successful people have used their minds over all things that matter.

> EVERYONE WANTS TO BE AN OUTLIER, BUT NOBODY WANTS TO BE AN OUTCAST.
>
> —CHRIS JARVIS

Generally accepted psychology tells us that most people want the same things. Maslow's hierarchy of needs says humans have basic survival needs like oxygen, food, and water. Then, once we have basic survival covered (Wi-Fi helps too), we need safety and security. The third need is for love and belonging. Often, this is referred to as "fitting in" and "being part of something." Most people want to be like their colleagues because they want to be liked by their colleagues.

MASLOW'S HIERARCHY OF NEEDS

Self-actualization
desire to become the most that one can be

Esteem
respect, self-esteem, status, recognition, strength, freedom

Love and Belonging
friendship, intimacy, family, sense of connection

Safety Needs
personal security, employment, resources, health, property

Physiological Needs
air, water, food, shelter, sleep, clothing reproduction

This third area is where super-successful people are most different.

Each of the billionaires and all the hundred-millionaires I have met or worked with have similar stories. When they had their greatest idea—and they all remember the one that changed their lives forever—they recall sharing it with friends, family, spouses, parents, investors, friends, or even colleagues and business partners. Without exception, every one of them was told that their groundbreaking idea was absolutely crazy, too risky, or downright foolish.

If you are anything like I am, you have had countless wild ideas. On some level, every human does. The ability to imagine something we can't see and remember our ideas is one of humankind's major evolutionary advances. Among us, the levels of success we achieve are determined by what we choose to do with these ideas.

When you share your ideas or dreams, you probably get similar responses. It isn't the idea or the criticism that made the super-successful people different. It's what they did with the feedback. Without exception, every one of them completely ignored all the criticism and pressed on with the big idea. They were made fun of, laughed at, and even shunned in some instances.

They resisted the urge to fit in and fall back in line; they left the herd and became a giraffe.

Why did they press on with their big ideas? They pressed on because they had a vision of what they wanted out of life, and, more importantly, they decided they didn't need anyone's approval. People who earn millions of dollars per year are unlike 999 out of 1,000 people.

Most of us want to be outliers financially but are not willing to be outliers socially. It's okay to want to fit in with a group of people, but that is not how you'll achieve your greatest levels of success.

I'm not saying you need to be antisocial to be successful. You need to focus on what you want and not let other people's commentary impact how you feel about yourself, your dream, or your path. This new path may

WHAT DO YOU GET WHEN YOU MIX A DOG AND A GIRAFFE?

AN ANIMAL THAT BARKS AT AIRPLANES!

be the less-traveled one; in fact, it may well be a never-traveled one. Remember, the herd's single function is to preserve most of the group. Any idea that suggests splitting up will be seen or felt as a threat, so you can't expect others to respond favorably to any innovative idea you have.

Traveling on your temporarily lonely path is where you will see the most growth.

FOR BUSINESS

In my thirty-year career in financial services, I attended hundreds of industry conferences where multiple companies, distributors, and salespeople would gather to discuss products, industry changes, regulation, and market opportunities. When my firm represented hundreds of medical practices, I had the opportunity to speak at countless medical association meetings, where competing physicians in the same specialty would share research, best practices, and practice development ideas.

As a competitive person, it struck me as odd that people would share their ideas with colleagues and competitors.

Then, it became clear that the industry's fear of not surviving is more powerful than the desire to thrive. Even in competitive industries, the herding mentality is unavoidable. It is with humans as it is with all animals: It is part of our DNA to do everything we can to survive. Nearly all our instincts are attached to either personal or special survival. The problem is that playing it safe devolves into mediocrity, especially in business.

After the TEDx Talk I gave in 2022, the popularity and viral nature of it made it clear to me that, after the COVID-19 pandemic, people were struggling to find their place in life and business.

The biggest misconception in business is that "playing it safe" is actually "safe." Doing what appears safe at the time, like following the asses in front of you, will reduce the speed of your decline in the short run, and put your business at greater risk in the long run.

In the lifecycle of a corporation, companies become successful because they: 1) innovate, 2) scale, and then, unfortunately, 3) preserve. This natural 1-2-3 progression is problematic due to the ever-changing shifts in culture. Step 2 requires systems, processes, and protocols—things that often alienate the founders. When those "big idea" people leave the company for a new venture, there is nobody left to help the company innovate again.

A better model is: 1) innovate, 2) scale, then go back to 1) innovate.

A sign that your company is in decline is that the human resources and legal departments have a significant impact on the operations and management of the company. This is a sign that a company is preserving what it has rather than finding new ways to innovate so it can continue to grow.

In 1997, I met one of my early mentors, Hunt Ramsbottom. I was in business school at UCLA and had earned a scholarship from the Young Presidents' Organization (YPO) for entrepreneurial achievement.

When Hunt's private equity firm was acquiring companies within the same industry to merge and consolidate them, known as a roll-up, one of the first things he did was fire the senior management team. He didn't do this because they were not good at their jobs. He did this because these executives were generally experts in their industry. Why did he fire them? His goal when executing any roll-up was to innovate and to create significant value from that major innovation. He told me that he never wanted to hear, "We tried that, and it failed," or "It doesn't work like that in our industry."

Hunt would bring in executives from very different industries. In one example from the automotive industry, he brought in executives and advisors from food and beverage, financial services, hospitality, manufacturing, and other industries. These executives were to come up with and execute upon ideas that other companies in his space would never think of doing.

Just like the crazy idea of an animal with a sixteen-foot-long neck, it worked wonderfully!

If you want to have more control over your success, find a way to do things differently.

If the thought of acting on your ideas scares the dung out of you, I have good news for you. You're normal. Now, be abnormal and move forward through the fear. *Be the giraffe.*

TODAY'S REACH

AVOID THE MASSES— THE "M" IS OFTEN SILENT

The herd animals on the savanna rely on safety-in-numbers to increase their odds of survival. These animals have no choice but to go along with the group mentality. If you were comfortable doing what everyone else wanted and going where others wanted you to go, you wouldn't be reading this book.

Giraffes are nonmigratory animals that have far more freedom to explore different habitats. To help you create similar freedom in your personal and professional life, there are a few things you will want to think about as you continue reading this book.

Start your days or your weeks by becoming more aware of where you are spending your time. Yes, this continues the last chapter's theme of getting your head out of the weeds. But wait, there's more! (It's not a second set of Ginsu knives, but I want you to dissect your answers.)

Sometimes, you may find yourself relaxing, while at others you are burning the candle at both ends. You may notice that you are spending significant amounts of time exercising, doing yard work, reading, study-ing, or walking the dog. Maybe you're checking emails during the evening, on weekends, or even in the outhouse. At these moments, ask yourself: Who am I doing this for? Is this something you want to do for yourself, because someone expects you to, or is there some other motivation?

Don't leave your curiosity at the door when you get to work. Lift your head and pay attention to what you do and why you do it. You may want to pay particular attention to interactions with employees, customers, and prospects. Perhaps the way you conduct meetings is predictable but no longer effective. What could be done differently to make work more efficient, effective, or fun?

When did you last review your marketing, prospecting, and sales pro-cesses? You may want to stop and ask yourself if there might be a better way to generate new business.

Don't be discouraged if you find that most of your activities are con-nected to other people's expectations or desires. It's great to be able to do things for others at home and work, but take time to understand your motivations and the costs associated with these activities. Giraffes are purposeful. We don't just take on projects and activities because oth-ers do them. And giraffes are very comfortable defying expectations. We want to start thinking about why we do things and what else we could do for ourselves and others.

What filled your schedule this morning?

What's on your plate today and tomorrow?

Why?

CHAPTER 3

BALANCE IS B.S.

DON'T GET A BIG HEAD,
UNLESS YOU HAVE A BIG NECK.
—CHRIS JARVIS

WHAT CAN FRONT-HEAVY GIRAFFES
TEACH US ABOUT BALANCE?

Obvious fact: Giraffes have large heads and long necks that are very dense and extraordinarily heavy. (That reminds me of the very dense, big-headed boss I had early in my career, but let's move on.) A giraffe's head and neck can weigh approximately 600 pounds. If you consider that the average weight of a male giraffe is 3,000 pounds, the head and neck make up 20 percent of his total body weight. By comparison, a human's head and neck make up only 8 percent. The difference between twenty and eight is significant, but that's only half of the story.

If you remember anything from physics or gym class, you know that the further you hold a weight away from your body, the "heavier" it is, in practical terms. You know the drill, hold a gallon of milk in one hand, close to your body. Then, extend your arm fully with the bottle in your hand. The same object exerts more stress on your body the further away it is. Back to wildlife biology.

A human head is centered between a person's shoulders and hips. The giraffe's disproportionately large head accounts for 20 percent of its total body weight and is way out in the front of its body. To say that a giraffe has a high center of gravity would be stating the obvious. A slightly less obvious, but clearly accurate, conclusion is that the giraffe is front-heavy. If it had evolved to become more balanced, it would have shortened its neck and given up its unique visual perspective and gustatory preferences.

To support this massively disproportionate weight imbalance, a giraffe's front legs are 10 percent longer than its back legs. This allows the giraffe to maintain its height advantage while not tipping over. There are other benefits this uniquely balanced animal enjoys too.

Have you ever watched sprinters in the starting blocks of a track meet? What do they do when they approach the finish line? They lean forward. Baseball and softball fielders are taught to have their weight on their toes, not on their heels. Basketball players are taught to have one foot forward in a "triple-threat" position so they can easily shoot, pass, or drive. Football players are all bent forward at the snap; every one of the twenty-two players on the field has his weight forward at the start of each play.

By leaning forward, it's easier for the giraffe to move quickly. This imbalance helps them get a quick start if they need it—in a race with an ambitious lion, for example. It also allows the giraffe to maintain a rather impressive speed of thirty-five miles per hour. It may look like a slow-loping animal, but the giraffe is one of the twenty fastest land mammals.

Last but not leaf (LOL), this imbalance allows the giraffe to stand on its hind legs to reach even higher leaves. Because there is so much weight in the front of the giraffe's body, there is little risk that the giraffe will fall backward while rearing up to reach higher.

FOR YOU

Balance is a very popular concept. Psychologists and therapists talk about having a work-life balance. Investment advisors talk about a balanced portfolio. Nutritionists espouse a balanced diet. When I stayed at the Miraval Spa & Resort, the menu whispered, "All proteins can be prepared 'Simply Balanced' with rice and steamed vegetables." Balance is a wonderful end result, but it is not the way to reach an ambitious goal. Why? Because nothing amazing can be achieved without some risk and sacrifice, which will put you out of balance.

Balance is a great idea after everything significant is achieved.

The problem is, like the body of the giraffe, our lives are never truly in balance. There is always something going on that we don't anticipate or don't plan. We may have a financial crisis that arises out of misfortune, or health emergencies that hijack all our thoughts ... in fact, quite literally, while writing this paragraph, I dropped my iPad and broke the screen!

Overall, you can strive to have balance in your life, but your days will not all be balanced. You will have to focus on areas that require your attention—when they require your attention. The best we can hope to do is create a long-term balance by embracing short-term imbalance. This is achieved by looking at progress over months or years and not being consumed or overwhelmed with progress over days or weeks.

A great example of this strategy comes from the entrepreneurial business strategy program, Strategic Coach®. Dan Sullivan created Strategic Coach® to help business owners identify what's most pressing in their businesses and to create strategies to reach higher levels of success. His program breaks a business owner's schedule into focus days, buffer days, and rest days. Focus days are the ones where you do what you are uniquely gifted and love to do. Buffer days are pain-in-the-ass days where you run errands and address items that do not make money. Vacation days span from midnight to midnight—with absolutely no work. No emails, no calls, no work. The goal is to maximize focus days and vacation days and minimize buffer days. (Tomorrow just became a buffer day for me at the Apple Store.)[5]

BALANCE IS A NEVER-ENDING CHALLENGE

Our lives are the sum of all the events that happen to us and the reactions that we have to them. For this lesson, we don't need to get into a metaphysical discussion about our roles in creating the events that happen in our lives. We need only acknowledge that some events require more time and attention than others.

For example, when my daughter was born, we didn't live near either of our families. As a result, I took the better part of a month off from work. Of course, I had something to do with having a child but, at the time of conception, I didn't plan to take weeks away from the office.

When I was running a consulting practice for wealthy clients, we would secure 90 percent of new clients in the last two months of the year—every year. This meant that we worked twelve- to sixteen-hour days in November and December. The trade-off was that I was never in the holiday spirit. When selling a business, as an entrepreneur or coach to business owners, the closer we got to the closing date, the crazier the hours were. The race to get everything done would often result in twenty-hour days or even all-nighters.

Balance isn't something we check off our task list—it's a daily endeavor. Ironically, staying off-balance and ready to adjust is the key to making the most of our days.

This giraffe mindset will help you not to be so hard on yourself and those around you.

CAN WE BECOME AWARE OF OUR TENDENCIES?

When I developed the Find Your Wild Factor Assessment, I wasn't interested in what people say their priorities are. I wanted to make people look at their actual behaviors. You can say your body is a temple, but maybe you treat that temple like spring breakers in an Airbnb. The gap between desire and behavior is where we help you set and reach your goals.

Speaking of spring break, years ago, I was asked to be the keynote speaker at the Empower Brokerage Sales Conference in Cancun. I had every one of the qualifiers take the Find Your Wild Factor Assessment. Most people found the results very interesting and helpful. One participant, Monica, took offense to her inner animal being an Eagle. She said, "Your report is wrong. I'm not an Eagle! I'm not about money. I'm a people person; I should be a Penguin."

Thankfully, she was willing to work through the perceived discrepancy with me, which helped me learn what my assessment really measured. (This example may also help you better understand your results and how you've made decisions to this point.)

Monica's parents migrated to Texas from Mexico. They worked hard to raise five children in a trailer south of the Rio Grande River. To say they were poor would be an understatement. She said they worried about finances all the time. I asked her when she last spent money frivolously on a luxury item she didn't need and she replied, "Never!"

I then asked Monica, "What if I told you that you're an "Eagle," because money is the dominant voice in your head and you can't make decisions without considering the financial repercussions they might have?"

"That makes a lot more sense!" she admitted.

The category in which you score the highest (health, finances, fun, relationships, career) on the Find Your Wild Factor Assessment may also be called the *Dominant Voice* in your head. Your behaviors demonstrate that, when given choices in life, you sacrifice your high score less often than any other of the other areas. Conversely, it's your natural tendency to first sacrifice your low score. This is also the area of your life that you are least likely to make a priority for yourself.

In other words, no matter what you truly desire, and no matter how pure your intentions are, your inner animal is probably calling the shots.

But, like the giraffe, you too can evolve.

BALANCE IS FOR TURTLES

After obsessing about money, career, or even fun, many see the antidote to be balance. It sounds good, but it's a very dangerous trap.

Unless you have accomplished everything you want and you have no ambitious goals left, the concept of balance is bullshit. I'm not saying that you can't have a balance of money, health, purpose, relationships, and fun. What I am saying is that the way balance has been presented to you is a big fat lie.

According to *The Cambridge Dictionary*, balance is: 1) the state of having your weight spread equally so that you do not fall.[6]

I enjoy not falling, but the problem with the popular idea of balance is the concept of equal. People talk about proper balance as a state when all things are equal. The proper amount of importance, or weight, given to each area of your life is going to differ by individual. This has nothing to do with the time you spend on each area of your life. It's preposterous to think that you could spend 4-5 hours of your day on your health, finances, career, relationships, and fun. You would drive yourself mad trying to do so. Your boss wouldn't be too excited about the four-hour workday any more than your spouse would want four hours of quality time daily.

I've never achieved balance. One year, my tax return reported that I made $2 million; I lost $500,000 the next. Over the last five years, I've seen my weight fluctuate by forty pounds. My mother-in-law's advice to my wife was to measure marriage over years, not over days, weeks, or months. She said, "Some years will be better than others. If you have more good years than bad years, you're doing pretty well."

It isn't that we can't have balance in our lives overall. The point is that we cannot have balance in our lives today, this week, or even this month. Over the course of a few months or a year, we can enjoy successes in each area of our life, but those months or years will not be great at the same time.

My dad used to joke, "Everything in moderation ... including moderation." Some thought he was being prophetic. I knew he saw moderation as a formula for mediocrity.

THERE ARE THREE KINDS OF PEOPLE—THOSE WHO LOVE MATH AND THOSE WHO DON'T

If you skipped the author bio (I often do, so don't feel bad), you may not know that I am a bit of a nerd. My mother (of all people) once said, "Chris, one of your greatest strengths is that you're much smarter than you look." Thankfully, she's right. I majored in applied mathematics and worked as an actuarial analyst for multiple insurance institutions.

The header for this section is not (entirely) to poke fun at people who struggle with numbers. I understand I was born with my math brain, so I'm grateful, not boastful. But, as a mathematician, I was taught to appreciate the importance of formulas, values, and efficiency:

$$1 + 1 = 2$$
$$2 \times 2 = 4$$

$19^2 = 361$ (Shout out to David Bloomer, Classical High School, whose room number was 361, but he painted 19^2 over it.)

In school, you get grades A, B, C, and D. Hopefully there are very few E or F grades. For most, A was the best grade. At some point, that wasn't enough. The nerve of my kid's teachers to give other children As.

Society has become so obsessed with numbers that we've lost track of anything that can't easily be measured. And the most important things in life don't have a numerical value.

Before you base your next decision on some number, do three things:

1. Verify it's accurate.
2. Confirm that it's important to you.
3. Identify what it would cost you (in other areas of your life) to act on this.

FOR BUSINESS

You may have heard of the 80/20 Rule, also known as the Pareto Principle. This is very common in finance and management. Simply put, the 80/20 Rule says that 80 percent of your results will come from 20 percent of your efforts. You could also say that 80 percent of your profit will come from 20 percent of your products or customers. What is much more important to note is that the remaining 80 percent of your efforts will only result in 20 percent of your profits or productivity.[7]

What are you supposed to do with this information? Many people just accept the fact that this is how life and business will be. Some accounts, products, and customers are going to be very profitable and well worth the effort. Most of the accounts, products, and customers will take more time and be more difficult, which will make them much less profitable. We will just

WHAT DO YOU CALL A ZOO WHERE THE GIRAFFES HAVE TAKEN OVER?

GIRAFFIC PARK!

have to kiss a lot of frogs so we can eventually find the proverbial prince. Nooooooooooo!!!! That is not the elevated perspective of the giraffe.

When you accept the status quo, you are moving back toward the middle. You don't want to move with the herd. Before you can live differently, you must see a different path for yourself. Before you see that better path, you must think differently. Don't accept the 80/20 Rule as a law of science, like gravity. Accept it as law of sociology. Society doesn't want you to be different. People in our society don't want to accept responsibility. You want to be successful. You will be different. You will want to be out of balance!

Aim for 20 percent of your accounts, products, or customers to give you 100 percent of your results. How? By firing the 80 percent who are wasting your time and keeping you from finding or developing more like the 20 percent you love. I've heard it said that if you can't say no, your yes is worthless. If you are trying to be all things to all people, you will end up being nothing to anybody—because you'll be out of business.

The question is: What are you doing well today that is stopping you from doing what you should be doing? This one is deeper. It can be applied to dating, projects, hobbies, careers, and countless other things.

If you don't buy it, just ask one of the wealthiest and most famous investors in history, Warren Buffett. With a net worth of $117.5 billion dollars, his quote, "Diversification may preserve wealth, but concentration builds wealth," appears to support our hypothesis.[8]

Let's Only Grow Four Apples Per Tree! Wait! What?

In the fourth quarter of 1996, Apple's revenues dropped 30 percent. In 1997, Apple fired CEO John Scully and hired co-founder Steve Jobs to come back and right the ship. Twelve years earlier, Jobs had been unceremoniously removed from the company. He was determined to do whatever it would take to make things right. Jobs reflected on his first year saying, "(We had) fifteen product platforms with a zillion variants of each one. I couldn't even figure this out myself ... How are we going to explain this to others when we don't even know which products to recommend to our friends?"[9]

Walter Isaacson writes in *Steve Jobs* that he screamed "Stop!" in the middle of a product meeting. "This is crazy!" The CEO then went to the whiteboard and drew a simple cross. He then wrote at the top of either side of the cross, Consumer and Pro (for professional). These represented the two classes of buyers. On either side of the horizontal line, Jobs wrote Desktop and Portable. These represented the types of products Apple would develop. Apple would create and market one product for each of the four segments.

Apple's return to greatness wouldn't be simple, but it would result from simplification. Apple felt this pain. They lost close to $1 billion dollars in Jobs' first year back. Luckily, Apple didn't change course. In the second year under Jobs, the company posted a $309 million profit. They were back![10]

THE BALANCE SHEET

One of the best experiences I had in business was being part of Vistage's Chief Executive Group. Vistage is a CEO peer leadership group that I joined to expand my connections and knowledge as a leader. For ten years, around a dozen CEOs in Austin met monthly to share and address our professional and personal challenges. We were not a herd, but a tower! (This is your hint for a quiz in chapter 6—where you will learn the importance of this).

One member, Franklin, provided a wide range of insurance and administrative services to municipalities throughout Texas and the South. The business was doing well, but he was losing money on his health insurance offerings. No matter what he did, he continued to lose hundreds of thousands of dollars every year. Company leadership assumed that, to compete, they must provide a full scope of services to their clients. Losing his ass in healthcare appeared to be a cost of doing business.

You win some, you lose some, right? Wrong!

Franklin needed to make a change and he began by asking his clients if they had any problem with him outsourcing his company's health insurance offerings. They were not only okay with the idea, but they preferred separating the bids for health insurance and other services.

He didn't pay someone to take this cash-sucking area off his hands. He didn't close the business and accept defeat to stop the bleeding. Franklin went out and found a successful health insurance administration company that wanted to get into the municipal market, and they paid a tidy sum for access to his client base. He partnered with someone who paid him for the opportunity to take out his trash. Within two years, a publicly traded company bought his business for around $10 million.

Franklin improved his balance sheet and peace of mind by un-balancing his portfolio of services.

Unbalance yourself and your company. Don't be afraid to turn your company on its head!

When surveying successful entrepreneurs for this book, I asked them how much time they spent on the "wicked cool, move-the-needle, special-sauce" aspects of their business. I was surprised and disheartened to learn that, even the most successful business owners, spent 60-80 percent of their week running their business and tending to necessary but uninteresting areas.

If this group of successful entrepreneurs scored this way, imagine how most struggling business owners and managers operate.

If you are a tech company, this might mean you spend a lot of time on operations, finance, marketing, legal, regulatory, or administrative tasks, rather than developing your amazing software or app. Conversely, if you are a logistics company that transports concrete, then operations IS the thing you must do well to be successful, but how can you do it better? If you are a payroll company, then regulatory, legal, and administrative functions are integral to your success, but are they keeping you from innovating?

There is a highest and best use for YOUR TIME based on your role as the business owner and based on your skills, abilities, and experience. Are you making the best of your most valuable asset—you?

TODAY'S REACH

REMEMBER TO BE YOURSELF AND BE A GIRAFFE

Earlier we learned that, when compared to a normal herd animal, giraffes have a strange body; their front legs are longer than their back legs and they bend backward to reach especially high leaves. A very long and heavy neck makes the giraffe front-heavy. Because of all this strange disproportionality, giraffes look different and move differently. Despite all these unique qualities, the giraffe still makes it all work.

To illustrate this, think about a time when health, yours or a loved one's, was more important than money. Perhaps you booked an expensive procedure or paid a lot for travel to be with someone. Now, think about a time when you sacrificed your health for money. Maybe you took a red-eye to save money or maximize your time. You knew you wouldn't sleep well, but the ticket was so much cheaper.

Over the next few days, you will make many decisions about how to spend your time and your money. Notice how the importance of different areas of your life can change. Sometimes, health may be more important. Other times, you may be more inclined to sacrifice your health by going out late with some friends or staying up to work on a project or to prepare for a meeting or exam.

In other words, instead of setting your priorities in stone, try setting them in mud. Sure, your feet will get stuck in them when you try to move, but they can move. This slight shift can be very freeing!

How can you get more comfortable with being flexible?

CHAPTER 4

SWIM UPSTREAM

I'VE PICNICKED AT THE TOP OF VICTORIA FALLS AND WHITEWATER RAFTED BELOW IT, BUT SAW NO NEED TO JUMP INTO A BARREL AND CONNECT THE TWO.
- CHRIS JARVIS

What can giraffes teach us about decision-making, focus, and mindfulness?

Can giraffes even swim? From an earlier chapter, we learned that giraffes are gloriously independent. From childhood, we know that we should always use the buddy system and we should never swim without a buddy. If we are following conventional wisdom, then we might conclude that giraffes don't swim.

Gloriously Independent + Need for Buddy System = Giraffes Don't Swim

I have never actually seen a giraffe swim, but this book is full of giraffisms that are contrary to popular opinion. To be safe, I had to do some research on this one. The first scientific evidence I stumbled across supported the fact that a giraffe could float. A giraffe on its back with a margarita and the world's longest straw is a great idea for some future *Be the Giraffe* merch. As much as I love the image, it doesn't answer my question. I found another group of experts who said it would be very difficult for such a top-heavy and front-heavy animal to do well in the water. I don't need scientists guessing; I can make stuff up just fine on my own. The search continued, rather frustratingly I might add, until I found something more definitive.

Based on the natural buoyancy of most mammals, a giraffe could "swim" twenty-seven miles an hour in a river flowing at twenty-seven miles an hour.

But seriously, in 2010, *The Journal for Theoretical Biology* published the most comprehensive research on the question. It found that the giraffe, despite being one of the twenty-five fastest animals on land, the tallest animal in the world, and the fourth-heaviest mammal, could actually swim. The caveat the researchers gave reminded me of my teenage children. Giraffes could actually swim ... if they were inclined to do so.

What kind of inclination are we talking about here? Sure, an adult giraffe would have to be in water that is over sixteen feet deep for its head to be underwater while walking on the riverbed or lake floor. Second, there's the more philosophical question: Why swim when you can just walk?

All rumination and kidding aside, whether the giraffe chooses not to swim or simply hasn't faced the necessity to swim (when David

Attenborough was watching, anyway) isn't that important. What is important is that the giraffe hasn't been doing something that it doesn't have a practical need to do. Evolution generally brings abilities that improve our odds of preserving the species.

FOR YOU

How does a giraffe out of water help us make important decisions?

From giraffes, we learned that you don't have to see something to know it could be true. I am not talking about metaphysical, supernatural, or religious beliefs, though they would all apply here. I am talking about the belief in your own ability.

There are no videos of giraffes swimming, but the absence of social media evidence does not definitively prove that a giraffe cannot swim. Why is this important to you? Because you want to be the giraffe.

Remember back to childhood. Had you considered that you could ride a bike before you did it? Likewise, could you have had the ability to catch a ball, play an instrument, sing a song, or tell a joke before you did? Did you know that you could speak words in another language before you took a course? ¡Claro que no! (Of course you didn't!)

Ironically, the first year my son Tyler was learning how to play the saxophone, it did sound a lot like wildebeests crossing the river and being devoured by crocodiles. Seriously, we would call it the "silence of the wildebeest" when he went to practice.

The giraffe lesson is that you don't have to know how to do something before you try it.

You could also accept the fact that you are capable of doing almost anything another human has done if you were so inclined to do so. Just because giraffes could do something doesn't mean that they would or should. They are rather efficient and deliberate in their movements.

How deliberate and focused are you on what you are doing? Think about your plan for tomorrow or the upcoming week, and ask yourself: I could do this, but should I?

When you think about your personal life and professional life, you may want to consider if you are doing something because you can, because you're good at it, or because someone else wants you to do it.

For twenty-five years, I provided creative financial solutions to physicians, business owners, and super-wealthy families—including five billionaires. At one point, a federal court judge described me as, "A Financial Fixer, the likes of which you read about in novels and see in movies." My problem-solving mathematician brain, coupled with my knowledge of legal, tax, and financial strategies, made me a rather formidable asset for any wealthy family or successful business. The pay was great, but I lost interest and excitement in doing the same thing. And yet, I kept doing the same thing over and over again.

For almost ten years, I continued doing what others wanted me to do while foregoing my true love—helping entrepreneurs build their companies and improve their lives. In the opening chapter, I observed that the universe gives us subtle hints—and when we don't take them, the hints become a lot less subtle. I started down this path after my sister passed away. Still, it wasn't until I lost my business partner and my father in the same year that my giraffe sense of clarity kicked in, and I finally committed to finishing *Be the Giraffe* and building Giraffe University and Beyond Wealth to help transform businesses and the people who run them.

FOR BUSINESS

In the 2004 book, *Blue Ocean Strategy*, authors W. Chan Kim and Renee Mauborgne define the blue ocean as "unexplored market areas" where there wouldn't be so much blood in the water from all the cutthroat competition.[11] I like to think that giraffes were the original animals to play in the blue ocean.

You don't have to follow any competitor's lead. You don't even have to play by the rules that are common in your industry. Am I suggesting that you "cheat" in business? Yes! Of course, I am not suggesting anything illegal or unethical, but I insist you do something different, unconventional, and unexpected. This reminds me of one of the biggest mistakes I see when I speak at large conferences.

People come to conferences to get ideas for themselves and their companies. What a terrible idea! If your goal is for your business to be in the middle of the pack in your industry, you should attend industry conferences, watch what other people do, and then mimic them. If your goal is to dominate your industry or to double or triple the size of your business, you must think more like a giraffe. Do something nobody has ever seen from a company in your industry or of your size or in your location—be the swimming giraffe!

Go to conferences with your neck held high and learn what not to do this year by watching the migration of the herd. Go to industry events and be inspired by speakers and case studies—but don't copy them. Use their examples as inspiration for brand-new crazy ideas!

Think about any race—running, cycling, NASCAR, Iditarod, you name it. If your competitor has a lead and you both go the same speed, you'll never catch up, much less surpass them. Your business race is no different. Even if you figure out how to do exactly what they do at the same margin, and they don't ever improve (which is unlikely), you still can't win.

"But Chris, what if I work harder? I could use the Iditarod strategy, simply not sleep, and we'd catch up."

Wrong, giraffe-hopper. You'll crash and burn, freeze actually, and so will what's left of your team. In fact, this approach will guarantee you have a giraffeless team.

To grow significantly and gain market share, you need to play and win a different game. You need to *Be the Giraffe* that swims while the others run. What pool do you need to jump into to get there?

You may have heard that the Apple computer was not for business use when people thought there would never be a reason for individuals to buy computers for personal use. E*TRADE went to low-cost trades when brokerage firms were making a fortune on stock trades. Here are two specific examples that I love:

THE SAFEST CAR COMPANY PLAYING IT UNSAFE?

Have you ever heard of Overseas Delivery by Volvo? When the big disruption in the auto industry was to adopt "no-haggle pricing" to combat the negative experiences consumers were having at dealerships, Volvo went the extra mile. You can order a new Volvo and be flown business class to Sweden to tour the factory, test drive your car on their track, and tour Sweden. While everyone else was trying to remove the negativity in the car-buying experience, Volvo decided to turn the awful car-buying experience into an experience their customers would never forget. [12]

GIVE THAT GIRAFFE A MOP

While attending UCLA, a recent alumnus came to speak to our class about his commercial janitorial company. He was providing custodial services to schools, hospitals, and class-A office buildings. Seems more like a Dirty Jobs episode than an MBA speaker, but he taught me an invaluable lesson. He said that the smartest people in his class competed for the sexy jobs in investment banking and management consulting. There's a lot of competition in those industries.

He explained that he ran a commercial janitorial company. He was competing with former custodians and property managers who may or may not have finished high school or college. He attended Stanford for undergrad and UCLA for his MBA. He pointed out that his industry is not sexy at all—but it's very profitable. Don't be afraid to ignore the brass ring everyone is reaching for and find your own somewhere where nobody else is looking.

Wow. That's giraffe-y!

A POLICE OFFICER HAPPENED TO NOTICE A CAR ZOOM BY, AND IT WAS FULL OF GIRAFFES.

YES, IT WAS A CONVERTIBLE.

HE PULLED THE HUMAN DRIVER OVER (EVERYONE KNOWS GIRAFFES CAN'T DRIVE ... OR CAN THEY?) AND SCOLDED HIM.

"I DON'T KNOW WHAT YOU'RE DOING WITH THESE GIRAFFES, BUT TAKE THEM TO THE ZOO RIGHT NOW!"

"YES, OFFICER," HE REPLIED AND WENT ON HIS WAY.

THE NEXT DAY, THE POLICE OFFICER SPOTTED THE CAR AGAIN, STILL FULL OF GIRAFFES, NOW WEARING SUNGLASSES.

PULLING THE DRIVER OVER AGAIN, HE YELLED, "I THOUGHT I TOLD YOU TO TAKE THESE GIRAFFES TO THE ZOO!"

"I DID, AND WE HAD SUCH A GREAT TIME. TODAY, WE'RE GOING TO THE BEACH!"

In business school, we had marketing classes that frustrated me to no end. They were all focused on marketing for big consumer products companies like Proctor and Gamble, General Mills, 3M, etc. Every class was about the 3 Cs and 4 Ps—or was it 4 Cs and 3 Ps? I went and looked it up for you. The 4 Ps of marketing are Price, Product, Place, and Promotion. There are, in fact, 4 Cs: Customer/Consumer value, Cost, Convenience, and Communication. Because so many of the marketing majors in my program went out to work for large companies like General Mills, Proctor and Gamble, and others, customer surveys and focus groups were huge parts of the curriculum.

This approach was torture for this entrepreneur.

I started a company very early in my MBA Program. At the beginning of the second quarter of a six-quarter program, I partnered with an attorney and fellow MBA from UCLA to launch Guardian Publishing, a marketing company that helped pharmaceutical, medical device, and professionals reach physicians through valuable financial and legal content we created. As an unfunded start-up, we bootstrapped everything. I was living on $2.50 burritos and cheap toilet paper (not a good combination, I might add) and couldn't afford to outsource expensive customer research. I had to make some sales to keep the lights on every month. Stretching a dollar to survive was my religion—and religion was not part of the curriculum at a top business school. Despite peers pulling for us to make it, it became obvious early on that we were on our own.

During our business plan competition, we got more of the same.

Nobody will work with you because everyone already has financial advisors. There is no need for another firm to do what you do. Doctors will never work with you. They have too many gatekeepers.

We heard all these critiques—and then some less polite ones. If we had taken everyone's advice about success in a conventional model, we would have chosen something else. We didn't. We had to test our hypotheses with live demonstrations and with actual client prospects. We wouldn't know what people wanted or how they wanted it until we got into real conversations.

Nobody had ever driven tens of thousands of leads from high-income medical specialists before. Nobody had done it by writing articles in clinical journals, speaking at clinical conferences, and from sponsorships from pharmaceutical companies. There was no beaten path to walk down, no one to follow. We had to walk from tree to tree. And it worked.

There is an exercise I like to do with companies during strategic planning sessions. An effective way to make companies stand out is to ask people,

"What do customers hate about your industry?"

For example, people don't like haggling with car dealers or dealing with health insurance companies for pre-existing conditions, prior approval, or negotiated co-pays. When it comes to car repairs and attorneys, people hate that the bill is always more than initially quoted.

Your mission, should you choose to accept it, is to identify:

- Something you dislike about your workplace or career and ask yourself to come up with some upstream solutions that might help the company and your colleagues, and therefore help you. Redesigning

TPS reports to make them more useful could be an example.

- Something people hate about your industry and brainstorm what the opposite action might be. Fixed-price cars (like Tesla) and flat-fee legal work would be two examples.

If you really want to go through some cheap toilet paper in a hurry, ask your clients what they hate about working with you. If you're brave enough to do it, this might change your life—positively!

The only way to stand out as a person or as a super successful organization is to do something that others would not. Say something differently, work with a group others would not, offer something others would not, offer something others might not think is profitable, or be there for someone in a way nobody else has. As you think about going places where those around you haven't been, realize that your inner circle can't give you sound advice on how to get there.

What are three things you have thought about doing but haven't because you were concerned what others might say or think about you?

Maybe it was taking dance lessons, learning to play the guitar, or joining an improv comedy troop. Perhaps you always wanted to learn a foreign language, go on a mission trip, or travel to some unusual locale.

If you are feeling up for it, write down at least three of those things and share each of them with someone. Yes, you can share each with a different person.

Then try some stuff. Run, fly, or even swim. Just don't float downstream.

CHAPTER 5

BEWARE: LIONS & HYENAS

PREDATORS ONLY TAKE ONE OF US PER DAY, WHICH IS GREAT—UNLESS YOU'RE THE ONE.

What can a giraffe teach us about avoiding problems before they get too big?

Giraffes are one of the heaviest mammals found on land, behind only elephants, hippopotamuses, and rhinoceros. To hunt such a large animal, a predator would need a great deal of size, strength, and optimism. In Africa, the two largest hunters of land mammals are lions and hyenas.

Given the significant size differences between these predators and our beloved giraffe, a single lion or hyena doesn't pose much of a threat to a healthy adult giraffe.

The key words are "single" and "healthy."

Let's look at the evolution of the lion. One path could have been for the lion to grow in size to be able to feed on large prey like elephants, rhinoceros, and giraffes. Did nature make a mistake? Hardly. If a lion evolved only to grow larger, the larger lion's body would have decreased stamina and agility, both of which are necessary for hunting smaller prey. That super-buff lion would also struggle to hide its size while stalking prey. If there is any doubt about this, look at who does all the hunting in a lion pride—the females, which are smaller than so-called kings. By growing larger, a lion would all but eliminate so many of its faster food sources, like impala, zebra, and wildebeest. Nature favors variety and flexibility, so evolution took the lion down a different path.

Lions also evolved into apex predators by learning to hunt in groups, called "prides." This allows them to work together to hunt much larger prey than one lion could ever hope to tackle. A lion pride may consist of one or more pride males, several lionesses, preadolescent males, and even cubs. These groups definitely pose a threat to even the largest walking buffet.

Hyenas are similar in their commitment to teamwork, but that is where the similarities between lions and hyenas end. Though hyenas are surprisingly expert hunters, they are more famously known as apex scavengers. Because hyenas work together in a "clan" or "cackle" of twenty to forty members, they can harass wild dogs, cheetahs, leopards, and even small prides of lions into surrendering their kills.

These dogs-on-steroids are cunning. They save energy and risk less injury by only having to hunt a third of their meals. This brains-over-brawn strategy could only happen in a female-dominated species. Unlike lions, the alpha in any cackle is always a female. She too can be replaced as the leader, but only by another in her bloodline, such as a daughter or a sister. You must be born into greatness and power in the hyena world.

Though not a serious threat to an adult giraffe, hyenas are not to be ignored. They live up to their reputation as master scavengers because they will take what matters most to a mother giraffe—her child. Leopards and crocodiles also hunt giraffe calves. [13]

On a related note: I hate hyenas.

FOR YOU

While small groups and individual predators can only take down newborn or very sick giraffes, prides of lions and clans of hyenas can take down elephants, hippos, and even healthy adult giraffes. This is why the most dangerous place for giraffes to roam is into a large, hostile group.

Like giraffes, we are reminded that there are some people, albeit few of them, who may want to deliberately hurt us. In the same way hyenas significantly outnumber lions, we will likely encounter many more jealous "scavengers" who want what we have. Giraffes remember that there are times and places where we are more vulnerable.

> "If you know the enemy and know yourself, you need not fear the result of a hundred battles. If you know yourself but not the enemy, for every victory gained you will also suffer a defeat. If you know neither the enemy nor yourself, you will succumb in every battle."
>
> — Sun Tzu, *The Art of War*

Our world, like the giraffe's, is full of predators and scavengers that we should take time to identify and understand. *The Oxford Learner's Dictionary* offers two definitions for predator:

Predator (noun)

(1) an animal that kills and eats other animals.

(2) a person or an organization that uses weaker people for their own advantage.[14]

Predators are significantly outnumbered by their prey—which makes sense because a large percentage of predators in any population would result in mass extinction. Though the small number of hunters does not threaten the total population, that doesn't minimize the severity of the situation for the one animal that is targeted.

There is a very small percentage of people who will try to exploit us or cause us pain. Because the damage they can cause us is so severe, it would be irresponsible to ignore the risk. The giraffe teaches us to keep an eye out for predators so we can avoid them before an encounter where we must defend ourselves.

On one end of the spectrum, you have the emotional predator, defined as someone who enjoys watching or causing pain in others. On the other end of the spectrum, you have the accidental predator. These people don't mean to hurt you, but interactions often end with biting.

A simple but weirdly untrodden path to more happiness in life is to spend less time with people who make your life harder—and more time with people who make your life easier or more enjoyable.

Picture our giraffe friends, hanging out occasionally but taking plenty of time to refuel while they take in the view.

EMOTIONAL EATERS

I'm not advocating labeling people as predators, but I'm also not advocating being naive prey. Let's start with the actively predatory people. The giraffe teaches us the value of identifying and calmly avoiding those predators by keeping a safe distance. This holds true for people and situations.

Many years ago, I went through a very messy divorce. Like most couples, we had certain topics that were hot buttons and would lead to petty comments or downright hurtful interactions. Though I've been remarried for over a dozen years now, seeing couples bicker and argue in similar ways still doesn't sit well with me. I wouldn't say that I feel I am responsible for helping them, but I know that it puts me in a vulnerable headspace. This is an example of how a certain circumstance can impact you.

Another example goes back to my twenties, in Rhode Island. My mother is a wonderful woman who has been the victim of bad luck. She has been divorced, remarried, and unexpectedly widowed, all before she was forty-five. My younger sister also struggled with undiagnosed learning challenges and diagnosed psychological issues. My mother was struggling with her own depression and the financial challenges of facing foreclosure. My sister was going through hormonal changes and crazy mood shifts from the psychotropic prescriptions, and her doctors were not communicating clearly with each other. To say that the environment at home had nothing to do with my decision to attend grad school at UCLA, 2,500 miles away, would be naive.

And the sad part is, stuff like this didn't just happen in my family. While teaching my Million-Dollar Advisor Two-Day Boot Camp, sponsored by Midland National Insurance Company, I learned an invaluable lesson from my attendees. While working through the "Removing Obstacles to Success" segment, these wildly successful financial advisors shared something about family and friends I wasn't expecting.

Ninety-five percent said that when they earned a big commission or landed a big client, they were met with significant negativity from people close to them. Everyone in the room admitted that they purposefully kept their success and income from people in their families to avoid snarky comments and jealousy.

How can your success not be impacted, at least subconsciously, by the attitudes and expectations of people around you?

Are there situations, conversations, or people close to you who aren't particularly positive, encouraging, or supportive?

If you have ever watched any of the famous movies that depict sales-people, such as *Glengarry Glen Ross*, *Boiler Room*, or *The Wolf of Wall Street*, or if you have ever worked in a high-pressure sales situation, per-haps on Wall Street, you know where I am going. These highly compet-itive environments resemble locker rooms, and your boss acts like an unhealthy mashup of Bobby Knight and a stereotypical drill instructor— complete with the loud voice, intimidating stares, occasional shoving of furniture, and an endless stream of derogatory comments.

These situations can break your spirit, but we aren't only vulnerable when someone in authority is taking advantage of us.

The giraffe reminds us that even the strongest of us can be vulner-able to the attitudes and actions of larger groups AKA the herd, or the mob. Think swarm of mosquitos. Today, anyone can share information on a wide range of social media platforms. As a result, we have been given lots of disinformation and misinformation. We often don't know what the hidden agenda might be. One example of this is the cancel culture that has arisen. People can be ostracized, or their lives or careers ruined, because of disinformation or misinformation about them.

The giraffe does not fear the king of the jungle, but it should be very worried about a pride of lions. And even a swarm of flies can make for a miserable day or month. We must also be very aware of the dangers of our own pride. *The Merriam-Webster Dictionary* gives us the definition:

Pride (noun)

(1) pleasure that comes from some relationship, association, achievement, or possession that is seen as a source of honor, respect, etc.[15]

"Good pride" represents our dignity and self-respect. "Bad pride" is a feeling of superiority that reeks of conceit and arrogance. You want to feel proud of yourself but don't want to compare yourself or look down on others. Similarly, you want to be happy with your own accomplishments, but you should never find pleasure at the misfortune or failure of others.

As it relates to pride, we can take responsibility for ourselves and still be sensitive to the feelings of those giraffes in training. We will learn the importance of encouraging others later, but the takeaway from this section is not to brag about our accomplishments in a way that makes others feel inferior. We want to be seen as giraffes, not sound like hyenas, don't we?

Am I saying you should only hang with other giraffes? Yes, whenever possible. Remember, the herd attracts predators and parasites. And they smell like shit. Just sayin'.

FOR BUSINESS

Like giraffes, businesses must face their own lions and hyenas. It probably makes sense to point out that the hunting lion is the animal out for itself and its pride by trying to win market share, make money, close the deal, and build their brand with little thought about the prey. The scavenging hyena is looking to take something that someone else earned so it focuses less on the fallen prey and more on the weaknesses of the hunter, whose prize is soon to be theirs.

If you run a fine dining restaurant or want to start one, you probably think about other nice restaurants as your competition. If you run a bookstore, you likely consider other bookstores as your rivals. Though you must pay attention to direct competitors, the giraffe teaches us that the most dangerous predators approach carefully and undetected.

> **HAVE YOU EVER SEEN ANY GIRAFFES HIDING IN TREES?**
>
> **NO.**
>
> **THAT'S BECAUSE THEY'RE SO GOOD AT HIDING.**

In this restaurant example, stealthy predators are everywhere, especially where you're not looking. The expansion of fast casual dining, food delivery services, delivery of prepackaged meals, and delivery of prepped meals has threatened fine dining. In other words, companies that ship high-quality ingredients to people's homes are a threat. All forms of entertainment are a threat because a major element of fine dining is the entertainment value of the experience, right? All restaurants face the challenge of simply getting people to want to change out of their pajamas and go out in public. So, what are you going to do about it?

One of the most valuable lessons I learned from a speaker was in a Vistage group meeting focused on the biggest personal mistakes made by entrepreneurs. He stated that, as entrepreneurs, we tend to hire fast and fire slow.

The explanation (an excuse, actually) for this is that we hire based on "what people have done" and fire based on "who a person is." The obvious takeaway is to hire slowly and ensure we truly understand who people are before we hire them.

NOT ALL WERE AS SHINY AS JADE

In the years leading up to the sale of my company, Jade Risk, we navigated some dangerous terrain. Our original business plan called for direct sales to business owners and indirect sales through financial advisors. I thought it would be a clever strategy to grow through the efforts of commissioned salespeople without having to pay salaries and benefits. I thought I was filling my karma tank too when I recruited great folks whom I had known for twenty years. Since they had financial challenges, I figured they would work extra hard toward a win-win scenario.

Relying on people who were backed into their own corners and not highly supervised was a disaster. An outside salesperson convinced my head of operations, as well as other independent salespeople, that they could take Jade's clients, put us out of business, and create a competing company. They went so far as to falsify documents to show Jade's outside investor in an attempt to create a distraction while they tried to hijack the business's clients.

My investor was furious with me when he heard the accusations. He threatened to shut down the company, walk away with a $500,000 loss, and let the hyenas have the clients. Luckily for me, he was a rational and diligent person. I asked for a meeting where I gave him power of attorney to review my financial accounts. He took his time and found that I was telling the truth, none of their accusations were true. This saved the company, but it was a horrible scare. Fourteen months later, he recouped his investment plus another million dollars in the sale.

I have shared this story with many of my clients, colleagues, and friends. Amazingly, many of them had similar experiences. The takeaway from this story is that, when you sacrifice your guidelines, principles, or morals for money, two results are almost assuredly guaranteed:

1. The money is always much less than you hoped.
2. The sacrifice is always much more than you feared.

TODAY'S REACH

Beware of hunters and scavengers who are looking out for themselves and who don't have any regard for who you are, what you need to do, or how important it is for you to be different. If personality conflicts are the biggest problems we face in our organizations—and in our lives—then we should be extra careful not to hire people, or be around those who have different goals, expectations, and values.

Make a list of the ten people you spend the most time with at work and out of work.

Then, ask yourself whether these people are a positive or negative influence on your life. Positive people are those with whom you would like to spend more time. Negative people are those with whom you would like to spend less time, whether that's practical or not.

What can you do to increase the amount of time you spend with positive people?

What can you do to limit the time, or the impact, those negative people are having on you?

Hanging out with an immature giraffe is way better than being in the company of even the most polite hyena.

CHAPTER 6
BUILD YOUR TOWER

THERE IS STRENGTH IN NUMBERS,
UNLESS EVERYONE YOU HANG
AROUND WITH IS AN IDIOT.

Why do we call a group of giraffes a tower—and why do you want to build your own?

We've already discussed the herds of buffalo, wildebeest, and zebra. Herd is an appropriately boring name. Other animals have much cooler names for their associations and congregations. A pride of lions—that's cool. Who wouldn't be proud to be among those rulers of the plains?

As you know by now, because you're enrolled in this zoology course, er ... book, hyenas are in a "clan" or "cackle." If you have ever seen hyenas surround, torment, harass, and scare another predator into surrendering its kill, you know how "cackle" is a fantastically appropriate name.

Imagine coming across a murder of crows. Do you think that might be where Alfred Hitchcock got the inspiration for his epic movie *The Birds*? What about a shrewd of apes?

Buffalo are called a "gang" or "obstinacy." A "crash" of rhinoceros seems appropriate. Is that better than a "stench" of skunks, "prickle" of porcupines, or a "leap" of leopards?

Okay, enough.

As stated, a group of giraffes is called a tower. When they stand next to each other, their necks and heads rise up to form what looks like a tower. Their bodies form the walls of the tower. I bet your friends and family won't get that trivia question right, try asking them.

According to *The Miriam-Webster Dictionary*,

Tower (noun)

(1) a building or structure typically higher than its diameter and high relative to its surroundings

(2) a towering citadel: FORTRESS

(3) one that provides support or protection: BULWARK
    a tower of strength

Tower (verb)

(1) towered, towering, towers

(2) to reach or rise to a great height

(3) to exhibit superior qualities: SURPASS
    her intellect towered over the others'

Synonyms: better, eclipse, exceed, excel, outclass, outdistance, outdo, outgun, outmatch, outshine, surpass, top, transcend[16]

What do you want from those around you? Protection and support seem like solid contributions. Why? The giraffe doesn't just want to just survive, it wants to strive! The tower helps you reach or rise to a great height by exhibiting your superior qualities. This is perfect!

A tower of giraffes can see in all directions at once, scouting destinations and paths others won't see. The tower will identify potential threats, and then vamoose, long before the herd starts to wonder where their pal Zeb went. With this foresight, the tower has time to plan for the future without taking time away from daily feeding. Their vision allows the young giraffes to follow the group's lead on how to live, where to look for food, and how to find other giraffes, providing protection and guidance to all its members.

FOR YOU

As humans, we are social creatures. To survive, we need others around us. A human baby that isn't held, nuzzled, and hugged enough may grow more slowly than usual. If this situation lasts long enough, the child can even die.[17] The fact that physical touch is important isn't a great revelation. What we learn from giraffes is that we don't need a lot of people, like the wildebeest and zebra do. We don't need just any people. We need the right people. A giraffe gets no benefit out of hanging out with an impala, buffalo, or zebra. Those animals have more limited perspectives and a downward focus most of the time.

Jim Rohn famously said that we become the average of the five people we spend the most time with. Are you happy with what that says about your future?[18]

The giraffe teaches us that we need to surround ourselves with people who help us elevate our perspective and see more. We need to surround ourselves with other giraffes! A tower! This is such a fitting name. When multiple, open-minded, visionaries look at a situation, they will provide different perspectives that will give the group a more comprehensive view of the situation.

Many aspects of life are better when shared with like-minded people. This shouldn't surprise us; we already get together on so many occasions.

1. Weekly religious services
2. Live sporting events
3. Sports bars
4. Birthday and graduation parties
5. Holidays
6. Weddings

The energy of a group, for good or bad, is undeniable. Part of the secret to long-term success and happiness is finding, or building, the groups that will encourage, promote, and support you in a positive way.

Another unsurprising, but sad, fact is that, according to a 2019 poll, one in four people reported they had no one to truly confide in. Nine out of ten people admitted that they downplay their feelings so as not to burden loved ones. There's a better way, my friend.[19]

TOWERING EXAMPLES

After working in the actuarial and insurance worlds for four years, where sharing feelings is not commonplace, I knew I needed a change. Rather than testing the waters in a new industry every few years, I decided to spend two years in a full-time MBA program at UCLA. I took out student loans, stopped working, and devoted the entirety of my time there to exploring new careers, industries, and fields while interacting with the over three hundred people in my class who were mostly in the same boat. This was a pivotal experience and helped me elevate my perspective considerably. I don't believe I ever would have figured out I was an entrepreneur or developed the courage to jump out and do my own thing if I hadn't gone to business school at UCLA.

Throughout this book, I talk about the challenges and epiphanies leading up to the sale of my company in 2016. I was so disenchanted with the financial services industry at the time that I decided to step back and look at my life and my goals. I committed to a year-long personal transformation journey that included multiple week-long in-person training courses with a cohort of sixty-five people and a couple dozen trainers. We had online training, weekly mastermind groups, daily interactions with accountability partners, and countless exercises to help us get our arms around what we really wanted out of life and how best to go about it. Once again, surrounding myself with people who had made similar financial and time commitments created the perfect environment for positive change.

When we connect with others, as part of our tower, we are exposed to different perspectives. With a better understanding of a complicated or emotional situation, we are more likely to make better long-term decisions.

Who in your life is a forward-thinking giraffe who helps elevate your perspective? Perhaps more importantly, who in your life is a small-thinking wildebeest whose opinions limit your exploration?

FOR BUSINESS

Giraffes build their towers with other giraffes, not zebras, elephants, or buffalo. Even though giraffes see more than any other animal, they only congregate with other giraffes who have similar perspectives. They realize that, on their own, they can't see everything at once and invite others to add to that vision.

Business can be very complex. The larger your company, the more markets you are in, and the more offices or locations you serve, the more complicated it is to successfully lead an organization. As such, there will be multiple towers you will have to build.

The most challenging new connections, and arguably the most valuable ones, involve really tall giraffes. You'll benefit most from more experienced, big-picture thinkers. If your company is big enough to have a formal board of directors that meets quarterly, and you can pay them for their advice and governance, you should do so.

Smaller companies or nonprofit organizations have volunteer advisory boards that can work very well. I currently sit on the advisory boards to the Dean of the University of South Carolina School of Medicine and for the IC^2 Institute at the University of Texas, Austin. These boards reimburse us for travel to the semi-annual meetings. The in-person meetings are supplemented with regular email updates, phone calls, and online meetings as necessary.

On the other end of the spectrum, there are groups of experienced leaders who work collaboratively. Examples of these include the Young Presidents' Organization (YPO), the Entrepreneurs' Organization (EO), and Vistage, to name a few. These groups may have a chairperson who leads the meetings, but the purpose of these groups is to create a collaborative, interactive team where the members provide experience and insights to the other members of the group. Though I was awarded a YPO scholarship when I was at UCLA, I was unable to grow my company large enough to qualify for YPO before I turned forty.

I turned to Vistage, where I was a member of one of Austin's Chief Executive Groups for over ten years. This was an amazing experience both personally and professionally. The group disbanded, primarily because most of the members successfully sold their companies and we no longer fit the criterion for membership, but the connections we developed have sustained us long after.

> TRUE STORY. A TOWER OF GIRAFFES WALKED INTO A BAR.
>
> "A ROUND OF LONGNECKS?" THE BARTENDER ASKED.

If you are just starting out or are looking for a change in your life, you don't need a formal group. You should look for mentors who can guide you. I have found that successful people are willing to advise inquisitive, respectful people. This was true for me both in the business world and in my former academic life. You can gain mentorship from a wide range of successful people if you respect their time and are flexible in how and when you will meet with them.

GIRAFFE-Y WAYS TO GET ADVISORS AND MENTORS

Perhaps you don't have the money to pay for an advisory board or to join one of the formal groups that can cost a couple thousand dollars per month. One thing you can do is reach out to experts in your industry and offer them advisory shares. I have assisted a half-dozen businesses in the financial services space in return for either a small amount of equity in their business or for some valuable promotion or referral they could make for me.

In my situation, when someone gave me a piece of their company, I always felt obliged to do something more for them. In the case of one wealth management firm, because I was so impressed with their investment returns, I sent them two of my clients for money management services. In the case of a health-tech venture studio, I returned the favor of their equity by introducing them to potential investors, including the most influential practice management consultant in the country. In the case of yet another client, I allowed the CEO to co-author an article that *Forbes* magazine had asked me to write.

The people you surround yourself with are going to have an impact on your life. How much impact they have, and whether that impact will be positive or negative, is entirely up to you. Once you find these trustworthy, heart-centered giraffes, it's up to you to create situations where they can have a positive impact on you, your career, your finances, and your well-being.

Imagine and describe the person you want to be—personally, professionally, or both. Then, identify people in your life, or the people you want to be in your life, who have these qualities. Ask them to lunch, breakfast, or coffee for a discussion. Tell them you respect them and would like to ask their advice.

Another method for identifying people who can advise you is to start by listing the difficult decisions or significant challenges you face.

What person, persons, or groups of people faced similar challenges successfully?

Ready? Now it's time to take action. Who will you contact today to build your tower?

There is strength in numbers but a special kind of power with your tower.

CHAPTER 7

BE A HAPPY NOMAD, BUT NEVER BE ALONE

I LIKE MAKING PLANS,
BUT I LOVE CHANGING
THEM INTO BETTER ONES.

What can giraffes teach us about leadership, innovation, and embracing change?

Giraffes are social animals, but they are not territorial. They roam across savannas, woodlands, and grasslands throughout many of the sub-Saharan countries in Africa. The path is different and completely unpredictable for each giraffe. A giraffe changes course based on its assessment of the availability of water and food, the presence of humans, nearby giraffes or predators—and the availability of a really tall chiropractor.

Contrast this to the zebra and wildebeest. These animals migrate along a very predictable pattern through the Masai Mara National Game

Reserve in Kenya and the Serengeti National Park in Tanzania. This 1,200-mile annual round-trip migration may be like some of your family's vacations, in distance and in drama. We once had six people crammed into a station wagon for nineteen hours, from Rhode Island to Hilton Head Island. Long before anyone mandated "No child left behind," we stuffed my youngest sister Jen behind the cooler and luggage "in the way back" of our vehicle.

Our vacations are a lot like the great migration in that both species are always looking for food. But the first big difference between the two journeys is that, as humans, we usually go on vacation to see something new or to quickly change climates; either way, it's a big change of scenery. Herds of epic migrators spend nearly 2,000 kilometers moving from one grassy plain to another.[20]

The second big difference is that we hate it when it rains on vacation. Migrators don't just walk to the rain, they run to get the freshest salad. The third difference is that traveling is usually the miserable part. Perhaps you've heard the phrase, "Life is a journey, not a destination." This must have been written by a zebra, or a wildebeest. Their whole trip is the journey, complete with crossing crocodile-infested rivers and navigating lightning-sparked fire. Every. Single. Year.

The fourth and final difference is the craziest. We all know what a pain in the butt it is when our children act like babies when they don't get their way on vacation. With zebras and wildebeest, most females give birth to a new baby on the trip. When was the last time you went on a vacation and came back with a new kid?

Giraffes eat tree leaves, and trees need water, so you might think the territories overlap. Surprise! We touched on it earlier, but since trees grow roots that are often as deep as the tree is high, trees can access water from underground aquifers in areas that don't have enough surface water for grass to grow. This is why we see pictures of thriving trees in deserts or plains where the grass is dead or dormant. The giraffe can survive in areas where other herbivores would starve.

The giraffe's ability to live without a herd gives it a great deal of freedom and allows it to survive in areas where other animals would not. They might go north when the masses are headed south, or just have a staycation in a grove of acacia trees on the side of a rocky hill with a great view.

As J.R.R. Tolkien said, "Not all those who wander are lost." This is true of our tall friends. Giraffes always seem to find each other. Obviously. Otherwise, they'd be extinct. The giraffes go on their own individual journeys to find what they're looking for. They are nomads, but are never truly alone. Private, but not isolated. Sounds like a nice vacation, and a great way to live!

FOR YOU

Do you feel trapped even though you're constantly moving around and busy? Do you feel like you are living someone else's life? Are you constantly comparing yourself to others at work, when you're with friends or family, or when you're scrolling through social media? Are you on a path your parents or peers selected for you? Are you afraid to end a relationship with someone who is no longer right for you? Have you held off on doing something you really want to do because you're afraid of what people might think about you?

It's human nature to wonder what other people are doing and where they are going. Peer pressure can be tough to ignore, and social media has severely complicated things for all of us. This is why we must look to our friend the giraffe. Throughout Africa, giraffes encounter millions of other animals eating grass and following the rains as they migrate. It's in a giraffe's nature to look, but not follow.

While millions of herbivores are eating grasses, giraffes are happy sticking to their tree leaves. When the herds leave to follow the rains, giraffes do not feel compelled to follow. No matter how many snorts, hoof stomps, or side-eyes they get, the giraffes trust that they are the ones with the best view of what will work for them. They will continue to assess the situation with their own two eyes and course correct when necessary.

From giraffes, we learn to live our lives. Our lives. The giraffe does whatever is best for its health and survival and, in the case of mommy-giraffes, what's best for their ten-foot-tall toddlers. As a kid, being taller than everyone else made me self-conscious. Giraffes stroll proudly because they are confident; they see the big picture, have a clear vision of the goal ahead of them, and can see the best path to reach it.

Unlike many humans, giraffes are very flexible. If it sees something unexpected, a shortcut or potential danger along the way, the giraffe will adjust course and strut its strange stuff in a different direction. Compare this to the stubborn wildebeest and zebra who have no choice but to stick to the plan and finish what they started even when that requires them to sacrifice hundreds of their herd in crocodile-infested river crossings.

How would you like to live knowing that your itinerary will be the same every month and every year for the rest of your life? Sounds like herd hell.

How about enjoying the company of other big-thinkers who never pressure you to follow? Better.

EVER HURT YOURSELF ... JUST TO BE RIGHT?

As a kid, I was smart enough to do well in school without having to work too hard. I guess I was lucky. But we all know luck goes both ways. Because I did well, I was never diagnosed with ADD or any other focus issues.

I got all As except for my C in penmanship and my D in Deportment. Like many undiagnosed or untreated children and adults, I was inquisitive about ... almost anything. Squirrel! Giraffe! I can still hear my father saying to me in high school, "You are great at starting new things, but you aren't great at finishing them." He wasn't wrong, and I know he didn't say it to be hurtful. He was one of the most driven and disciplined people I've ever met. He pitched for the Boston Red Sox and, if he hadn't hurt his shoulder during his military service in Vietnam, he might have had the hall-of-fame career he visualized.

Fast-forward to my career as an actuary. (Pop quiz: Who's more boring, the herd or the herd's accountant?) I knew I wanted more than to become an insurance executive, but my father's voice in my head reminded me that I didn't want to quit before I finished all my certifications. When I was separated from my first wife, and we both knew it wouldn't work, I heard that same voice in my head, reminding me that I didn't want to give up. I'm not blaming my father for any of my delayed decisions. I'm acknowledging that I often thought about what I perceived other people might think about my decisions or actions.

Ironically, my overactive brain was derailing my personal evolution. First, my perceptions were often wrong. Second, and more importantly, other people's perceptions of me shouldn't have mattered.

"What someone thinks of you is none of your business," said the Sage Giraffe.

Is there something you didn't, or don't, want to do, but you continue to do it to make someone else happy?

DAD'S GREAT REDEMPTION

Dad didn't need redemption, but everybody loves a comeback story, especially the crocodiles who wait nine months in that river. We struggled with our relationship throughout my teenage years. As a father, I now realize how much I contributed to those challenges. He became a great father and friend to me from the time I turned eighteen. Later in life, he became a rather Zen-like guide to me, his grandchildren, and many others. He told me something that I have shared many times, "Chris, you only live one life. You, and only you, are responsible for your happiness. If you aren't happy, you can only blame yourself if you don't do something about it."

What we learn from Ray Jarvis the Giraffe is that happiness is not a democracy. The same way a giraffe independently chooses its path, through woodlands, savannas, deserts, and across multiple countries, we have the freedom and independence to break free from the herd and live a life of our choosing.

The giraffe finds a place it likes and then naturally attracts other giraffes.

You have the strength and ability to leave that small town at the base of Killington Mountain in Vermont or that Dallas suburb to explore the West Coast or to try city living in Denver. The giraffe is never truly alone; it only embarks on its own journey to find what it wants before others find it. You'll only meet people who have a sense of adventure if you put your sense of adventure in motion. (To my niece Alyssa: This paragraph was written specifically for you.)

Freedom and flexibility are two things that many business owners, professionals, and executive clients of mine have told me they lack. Here's a great story of my client and friend Kevin.

Kevin is a middle-aged owner of a successful homebuilding company on the East Coast. He's married to Lori, a lovely woman who also works in the company, and they have two terrific daughters. As the company was growing, and everyone was putting in long hours to keep up with demand, Kevin was feeling guilty for taking time out of his schedule for himself. Specifically, he did not want to seem like a slacker by leaving early and he didn't want to be riding his motorcycle or taking guitar lessons while his wife was working late hours.

I shared my father's advice, which he liked, but it didn't assuage his guilt or change his schedule. I asked him to do two things: 1) Ask his wife if she minded that he started a new hobby or took Mondays off; 2) Ask his direct reports if they could move their weekly meetings to Tuesday or Wednesday.

When Lori encouraged him to do something for himself, Kevin set up his out-of-office on Mondays and none of his employees complained about the boss not being there. A couple of months later, I was speaking at Kevin's company meeting in South Florida. I apologized to Lori for convincing Kevin to start playing guitar around the house every day. To my amazement, she replied, "I am so grateful to you. It's the best thing Kevin has ever done for himself. He is happy before he plays guitar, and he is even happier after he practices guitar. He's a much happier person, and I'm so excited for him and for us. Believe it or not, he's become pretty good too!"

That's a lot of "happy" from one simple move, huh? And I'm sure you noticed that the happiness overflowed to his family, and I'd bet their employees appreciate Kevin more because he walks into the office every week a happier person.

I've made many choices in my life based on what I believed other people would think about me. I also know that I often did things based on a contract that no one else signed. In other words, I felt compelled to keep slogging, even though I hated the journey that nobody asked me to take. When my mom lost her husband, my stepfather, Tom I moved back into her house and paid rent to help her pay the mortgage. I assumed that she was my financial responsibility, and I was happy to help. When I had a chance to move to Boston to advance my career, she was the first one to say, "You need to go. I can take care of myself. Don't miss this opportunity!"

Had I not taken that and similar opportunities, which might have looked selfish to others, I wouldn't have been in a place of financial and schedule flexibility to help loved ones.

When we make choices based on what we believe, or hope others will think, we are giving away the power to choose for ourselves. We need to be more giraffe-like and do our own thing to make our lives work for us. Then, people who find us at our desired place in life will see the real us and not the person we were pretending to be. Making that change may seem difficult, but you will only be alone for a short while.

FOR BUSINESS

The giraffe teaches us that doing something different will require going out on our own and traveling without a clear destination. One of my best memories is the thirty-eight-day backpacking trip through Europe after college. Our best memories were as "accidental tourists," like when we stumbled into, and became part of, a rally for Vaclav Havel. We had no idea we were going to witness Czechoslovakia's first democratic election.

Though the path in business can be uncertain and sometimes scary, the giraffe shows us that you can—and should—expect to make many adjustments to your course along the way. Once you find a good place to stop, for a little while or for quite a long time, you're no longer alone because others will find you.

In my book 6 *Secrets to Leveraging Success*, I focused on the difference between successful people and super-successful people. We defined successful people as the households that make up the "1 percent"—American households with total annual income over $400,000. We then categorized the top 10 percent of that group, or the top 0.1 percent of households in this country. They earn at least $1.9 million per year.

What we found is that there are many clear paths to earning $400,000 per year—medical school, law school, certified public accountant at a big firm, or the owner of multiple franchises. However, there is no clear path to earning $1.9 million per year. Some, of course, were lawyers and doctors, but many had no college education. All of them were outliers financially and socially. They did things differently with little regard for what others thought of them. Remember Maslow's hierarchy of needs? He might say this was a breakdown of social construct, but who cares what that zebra-herder thinks, right?

Here's my takeaway, as someone who has consulted thousands of clients in the top 1 percent, top 0.1 percent, and top 0.01 percent: the super-successful are different in more ways than the outcome. They are different in their approach, and their different approaches have resulted in different outcomes. They are comfortable doing things others would never have considered doing.

When I sat down to write this book in 2019, I finished about 75 percent of it very quickly, then I put it down for almost four years. My dear friend, Jack Canfield, whose books have sold over 275 million copies, told me that *Be the Giraffe* was going to be a huge success and it would change my life forever. So, why did I let it collect dust for so long?

Although it is embarrassing, I'll admit that I skipped right past the excitement of what such a huge compliment meant. Instead, I thought to myself, where will all my clients go? How will I handle all their financial, legal, tax, and business needs? Admittedly, not very giraffe-y thinking for the giraffe guy.

I spent the better part of four years building the infrastructure to help these clients and sitting on boards of various financial firms to assess and expand their capabilities. I was fulfilling a contract nobody else signed. I didn't even ask my clients what they would do if I retired from financial advisory. So now, four years later, I am finally taking my own advice and doing what I love most—helping entrepreneurs start and grow companies that will change the world!

Remember when we talked about how the best ideas people had, the ones that led to their success, were often called crazy by family and friends around them? Gordon Logan, founder of Sport

> I ASKED MY DAUGHTER TO NAME TEN ANIMALS SHE MIGHT SEE IN AFRICA.
>
> SHE REPLIED: "NINE ELEPHANTS AND A GIRAFFE."

Clips, was a partner at one of the Big Eight accounting firms when he got his big idea. He told people he was going to start a sports-themed hair-cutting company for men and boys.

One of his partners told him, "Congratulations, Gordon. You just invented a barber shop, and there are already 50,000 of them."

Nearly all my clients shared similar reactions: You're crazy! What are you thinking? Do you want to lose everything? Why can't you be happy with what you have going on now?

Fast-forward twenty years, Sport Clips has over 2,000 stores nationwide. There are hundreds of franchisees employing tens of thousands of people. Gordon sponsors a NASCAR team and a NASCAR Race to raise money for veterans. He has created so much opportunity for so many people, given back to multiple causes, and he lives a great life. Gordon was the only member of our Vistage group who self-reported high scores for personal and business life every single month for over ten years.

He took nobody's advice, went out on his own, and he is not alone in any way now.

Lastly, I'd like to honor my good friend Jack Canfield. When he was pitching his *Chicken Soup for the Soul* book, he and his coauthor Mark Victor Hansen met with 144 publishers. Seriously, they got 144 rejections—people don't want to read about stories, it's a stupid title, who's going to take this title seriously?

With over 321 titles and more than 110 million copies sold in the US and Canada (and over 500 million copies sold worldwide), publishers now ask authors if there is any way to "chicken soup" the book they are pitching and turn it into a franchise. Jack and Mark went way out on a limb and ultimately changed the way publishing and storytelling were viewed. There are now countless workshops and consultants teaching "story selling." They were out on the frontier alone, but millions of book sales prove they weren't alone for long. [21]

TODAY'S REACH

Doing more and being more are phrases that both translate to being different. Different starts out with some loneliness. You will meet many people but will not be with them for the entirety of your journey. You may enjoy some of it together, but they have their own journeys.

When it comes to breaking away from people or responsibilities, consider these questions:

1. Where is some place you'd like to go but fear that people close to you might be critical or unsupportive? This could be physical, political, self-care-related, or professional.
2. What responsibilities have you taken on that need to be reviewed and renegotiated with other people?
3. What have you been afraid to do because you feared someone wouldn't approve?

Rather than focusing on what others might say, can you think of something about these actions that may make you happy or relieve you of some stress and anxiety?

The bad news, perhaps, is that multiple answers come to mind. The good news is that you only need to pick one action step. But you must pick now and take action today.

Hope to see you at a nice, leafy treetop sometime. Vaya con jirafa!

CHAPTER 8
STICK YOUR NECK OUT

NO ONE MESSES WITH ME,
BUT I NEVER GET A HUG EITHER.
—MS. PORCUPINE

What can giraffes teach us about betting on ourselves without ever gambling?

Evolution has done something unique for the giraffe. But before we get into this unlikely success story, it's important to understand some basics of evolution. Among other distinctions, we all know the basic category of animals: predator and prey. The unique traits and strategies of the predator and prey mean neither is ever 100 percent successful, and the most common protective strategy is to rely on safety in numbers.

Let's get off the dry savanna and find some shade. What do you notice when you look up at monkeys? They have evolved to become gifted tree-dwellers with long limbs, light bodies, thumbs on all four limbs, and a strong tail. These traits allow monkeys to quickly climb and jump between limbs and find safety in the treetops. Meerkats, warthogs, and other small ground mammals have developed strong claws and shoulders that allow them to burrow underground to avoid predators.

Not every individual survival strategy relies on avoiding predators. Some animals are not built for speed, climbing, or burrowing, so they must protect themselves in creative ways. A tortoise has evolved to have a hard shell that frustrates many would-be attackers. A porcupine has sharp quills that make it very difficult for an animal to bite it. Armadillos curl up on armor-plated skin. The Colorado River toad, marine toad, and the golden poison frog all release poisonous secretions to protect themselves from would-be predators. Toads that are brown or green are obviously trying to blend into their surroundings. Others, with bright colors or noticeable warts, choose to advertise, or threaten, what might happen if they were to be messed with. These animals found a way to be left alone in plain sight—like moody, hormonal teenagers in our homes.[22]

Whether a prey species has evolved to live predominantly in trees, burrow underground, or develop some type of shield, they all have one thing in common. Almost all herbivores have evolved to become less vulnerable; their evolutionary strategy and physiology minimize risk.

The giraffe is the only animal I have found that has evolved to become more vulnerable. The giraffe has the same seven vertebrae in its neck as a human does, but the giraffe's neck is as long as a man's entire body. And if you've watched any nature documentaries, you know the neck is the most vulnerable body part. At up to eighteen feet tall, the giraffe can't hide that vampire's fantasy from predators.

This vulnerability is unlike any other, but somehow it works because this vulnerability offers a unique advantage. As an herbivore, the giraffe spends most of its time eating. But unlike their grass-eating siblings, the giraffe feeds on the leaves at the top of the trees. You know this. But have you considered that it's a calculated risk? Increased vulnerability is a trade-off giraffes have gladly chosen. The benefits far outweigh the possible adverse outcomes.

FOR YOU

In the wild, many animals hide and run away from trouble. Others choose to scare off would-be attackers with colorful displays and poisonous secretions. From giraffes, we learn that there may be a better way to avoid undesired outcomes. Being able to outrun a lion, when your life depends on it, is a nice thing to be able to do. Running away or hiding from difficult situations or people is a short-term solution. By avoiding these issues, we don't resolve them.

The same way a giraffe can kill an attacking lion with a powerful kick, there are times when you must be strong and stand up for yourself. The giraffe teaches us that an aggressive attack isn't the only alternative, either. The giraffe evolved by sticking its neck out—this is a very different tactic from what other animals did. By being more vulnerable, the giraffe can see paths that others can't.

When dealing with challenging people or situations, we first must accept our responsibility in having allowed the situation to become what it is. By handling it a certain way—or not handling it, as the case may be—we've gotten ourselves into this predicament. Now, we need to focus on what we can do differently to improve our situation. And as you've learned by now, being the giraffe doesn't usually come naturally. It takes bravery and effort.

In the case of critical hyenas, you may want to remind yourself of the giraffe's majesty. As we'll discover, the way a giraffe walks can unsettle potential predators. Proudly stand up for and be yourself.

Initiate discussions rather than run from them. Share your thoughts and feelings. Most importantly, try to elevate your perspective to see the other person's view of the situation. This is a better path.

When I didn't get into Duke University, I begrudgingly went to the University of Rhode Island. For years, I had a chip on my shoulder that I should have gone to a better school. When I was applying to business schools, Stanford responded to my application saying, "You are at an academic disadvantage to other applicants. We do not recommend you apply again." This perpetuated what I already thought about myself. As I started writing books and conducting seminars, my subconscious motivation was to convince everyone how smart I was.

After doing many of the exercises in this book and in the *Be the Giraffe* video course, I became more aware of my insecurities. After taking the risk to survey attendees at my conferences, I found that the focus on my accomplishments made me appear unapproachable, which was the exact opposite of the result I wanted. One-on-one, I took great pleasure in teaching people from my mistakes, but something needed to change on stage.

When I exchanged the subconscious need to prove my intelligence for the conscious effort to show people how vulnerable I could be, something magical happened. My seminars became much more effective. I received higher scores, lengthy feedback, and was hired by larger percentages of the attendees.

It turns out that sharing my stories of struggling with my divorce, getting kicked out of my company, losing all my money, watching as my sister was over-

MANY GIRAFFES CAN GROW UP TO EIGHTEEN FEET. BUT MOST HAVE ONLY FOUR.

medicated to death, and fighting off suicidal thoughts didn't make me weak. My vulnerability had the opposite effect. People saw me as relatable, but they also saw me as strong and resilient for overcoming those challenges.

But there was one moment on stage at an insurance company's conference in Hawaii when I considered I might have left myself too vulnerable. While teaching this lesson and challenging the audience to be vulnerable in an area of life that was particularly difficult, a man in the back of the room raised his hand and asked, "What's a troubling area of your life and how will you be vulnerable to try and fix it?"

The first part of the question was easy. My wife Heather and I have a blended family. She brought Tyler and Kierstin, and I brought Chloe. As the kids became teenagers, the relationships grew more difficult. At that moment, in front of one hundred people, including my wife who was well aware of the struggles, I offered to adopt Tyler and Kierstin to demonstrate that I was serious about being their father, not just a fatherly figure.

That Christmas, one of their presents was a fancy pen, which they didn't understand. The next present was a set of adoption paperwork for each of them, already signed by me!

Putting myself out there in a way that demonstrated my love and commitment considerably improved our relationship. It's probably the best thing I've ever done for another person in my life, and I got to do it for two of my children.

FOR BUSINESS

There are human resources reasons, strategic planning reasons, marketing and sales reasons, and even financial reasons to increase your vulnerability.

HUMAN RESOURCES

A business is a complex set of interpersonal interactions. You have employees, managers, vendors, independent contractors, supervisors, and colleagues. You also have customers, clients, and distributors, and all those companies have people who will deal with many people at your company. You may have investors, bankers, and board members. Every person in each of those companies has ongoing relationships with a spouse or partner, parents, children, siblings, and friends. Every one of those interactions can be complicated.

When you consider how many interactions each person has per day or per month, you can appreciate how easy it is for drama and conflict to arise. The key is to create a culture that accepts this fact and promotes healthy ways of dealing with it.

STRATEGIC PLANNING

In 2007, Starbucks was experiencing its worst decline in the company's thirty-six-year history, prompting the return of the founder and original

CEO, Howard Schultz. When he returned, he didn't claim to be the savior. He didn't tell everyone that things would be alright. Schultz made himself extremely vulnerable to his employees, openly admitting how bad things were. He said that if things don't change, Starbucks would go out of business. His vulnerability and transparency were very well received, and the staff rallied behind him. Starbucks bounced back and built one of the most valuable and lucrative brands in the world.[23]

When I am asked to speak on innovation or to help a company find an innovative solution, I see the same problem over and over and over. Companies are too shortsighted. They are only looking at their closest competitors. As a result, they only see small or incremental changes. That's like a zebra looking for ways to improve by only looking at other zebras.

Who knows, maybe a giraffe is a prehistoric zebra who decided to stick its neck out and change its stripes! It's that out-of-the-box thinking that has led to some of the world's most creative acquisitions, such as:

1. In 2019, I consulted with an LED lighting company in Austin, Texas. Despite having lower prices than their competition, they were not winning accounts with their proposals. To circumvent the proposal process (where they were failing), we decided to partner with a low-flow toilet manufacturer. That may seem crazy, but the toilet company had a track record of helping its corporate customers reduce their water use. Companies don't replace toilets that regularly, so the LED-lighting angle allowed them to help their customers save another natural resource.[24]

2. In 2006, Google acquired YouTube for $1.65 billion. At my twenty-five-year business school reunion, my classmate Susan Wojcicki, former CEO of YouTube and Head of Google Ads before that, told us about the criticism she received for suggesting and completing that acquisition. Not all acquisitions go well, but Google makes more per month from YouTube ads than it spent on the acquisition.[25]

MARKETING & SALES

There are both traditional and nontraditional ways to think about marketing and selling—and of course learning from the giraffe. I am a partner in Mission 3A, a healthtech venture studio. When I'm raising money, people want to know about the downside. I tell them that every new venture has a risk of losing all the capital they invested. Since it is a tech company, we spend most of our money on coding and marketing, not on property, manufacturing, or equipment. If nobody buys our products, they will lose all their money. By sharing the downside of any investment, you build trust with your potential investors. Trial attorneys rely on a similar strategy.

You may not think of trial attorneys as marketers or salespeople, but they are constantly trying to win over the jury. What they say, how they say it, and when they say it are all important. A common strategy among defense attorneys is, "Let the jury hear the worst stuff from us, not from the prosecution." This is much better than a bombshell revelation being dropped on them close to their deliberations. In this example, being vulnerable by sharing potentially damning information may build trust.

My first company enjoyed a great deal of marketing and sales success, affording me the opportunity to share the principles of *"Giraffe Selling"* with audiences around the world. Nearly twenty years ago, af-

ter speaking to the MassMutual Greater Houston, CEO J.K. McAndrews gave me a gift that is making its way into this book today, a paperweight that still sits on my desk.

WHAT WOULD YOU ATTEMPT IF YOU KNEW YOU COULD NOT FAIL?

The best part of this question is that it gets you thinking about what you would do, why it would be important, and what it could do for you and others. Nowhere does it offer any qualifying statements or suggest any cautions. The answer to this question tells you exactly what you would want to do if you didn't have to worry about the downside.

When I finally gave this question long, hard consideration and accompanied that pondering with over five weeks of meditation, I made the decision to dedicate myself to finishing this book and related resources to help you *Be the Giraffe*.

Whether at work, at home, or with extended family or friends, I bet you already know an area that would benefit from vulnerability.

You know it because the thought scares the dung out of you, right?

What's sorely lacking in a valuable personal relationship? What could you share that would begin to fill the void?

What new problem does your company want to solve? If you have no clue, admit it and ask for help.

Someone might go for your throat, but you'll be able to shake them off and your tower will ride to your rescue.

Being yourself isn't a gamble because no matter what other people do, you win.

CHAPTER 9

HAVE A HUGE HEART

DO YOU WANT A BIG HEART OR A BIG BRAIN? YES, PLEASE.

What can giraffes teach us about getting the most out of ourselves and out of others?

You're this far into the book because you want to elevate your perspective and see better paths to health, wealth, and happiness. Either that or you're a clever lion looking for new hunting strategies. You may be wondering: What does the heart have to do with the giraffe's abilities to guide me?

Here's a quick and simplified anatomy review:

1. Mammals breathe oxygen into their lungs.
2. The heart pumps oxygen-rich blood through all parts of the body.

3. The brain is the biggest consumer of oxygen. Despite being only 2 percent of a human's body weight, the brain uses 20 to 25 percent of our oxygen.[26]

You're making the connection, aren't you? Heart Power = Brainpower.

Consider that a human heart pumps oxygen-rich blood less than two feet to our brains. The giraffe's heart must be strong enough to pump blood seven feet upwards to reach its brain, in addition to bumping it up from four long legs below. To accomplish this Herculean task, a giraffe's heart is two feet long and weighs about twenty-five pounds. By comparison, the human heart weighs eight to twelve ounces.

The giraffe is much larger than a person, so relative size is a better measure. Pound for pound, the giraffe's heart is more than twice the size of a human's. Without such a huge heart, the giraffe couldn't support a long neck. Without the long neck … well, you already know some of those perks. The giraffe's huge heart is the secret evolutionary advantage that supports these key giraffe attributes.

FOR YOU

When you took the Find Your Wild Factor Assessment, some of your lower scores may or may not have surprised you. If you read the personalized nineteen-page report you were emailed after taking it, you learned that everything we do in life is a tradeoff. Until this point, you have sacrificed the areas with lower scores for the areas at the top of your list. Whether this was a conscious effort or the result of subconscious conditioning is irrelevant. What is important is that many people may want different outcomes such as a higher score in one or more areas or a different hierarchy of your categories. To achieve this reprioritization in your life, the giraffe motivates us to elevate our own perspectives so we can find the secret to evolving and enjoying what we want.

In the amateur veterinarian anatomy lesson at the beginning of this chapter, you learned that the giraffe requires an enormous heart to pump so much blood up their long neck to reach their brain. Without this giant heart, the giraffe would lose its vision and perspective. With a proportionately sized heart, relative to its body, the giraffe would have to hold its head below its shoulder so gravity would bring blood to the brain, instead of keeping blood from getting there. Interestingly, the heart is the secret to the giraffe's ability to see what others can't.

Like the giraffe, our secret weapon is our heart. We don't need to wait millions of years for our hearts to double in size. We can lean on our hearts to improve our vision of a better life by adding greater weight to relationships and projects that touch our hearts.

We can also benefit by listening to our hearts more often.

In 2009, Simon Sinek became a household name when his "Start with Why" TEDx Talk went viral, reaching 10 million people.[27] His premise was to point out that individuals, as well as businesses, flourish when they have a strong understanding of why they do what they do. During my research, I found countless studies showing that having a clear sense of purpose has positive impacts on humans. Unsurprisingly, multiple sources connected a lack of purpose with multiple negative results.

HOW COULD YOUR SENSE OF PURPOSE IMPACT YOUR HEALTH?

- Mental & Emotional Health. With a sense of identity and enhanced self-worth, individuals report less stress, depression, and anxiety than individuals who claim to be searching for purpose. Those with purpose appear to set more ambitious goals, be more engaged at work, and report greater motivation.

- Engagement & Motivation. Without purpose, there is an increase in apathy and disengagement. These are precursors to depression.

- Coping & Resilience. Feelings of altruism and being involved in something greater than yourself provide increased motivation and more positive responses to obstacles and setbacks. Since the opposite of altruism—anomie, or feeling like you don't belong—is strongly connected to depression and anxiety, one would expect lower incidents of those feelings within people who feel connected.

- Belonging & Connections. Purpose-driven people report having stronger connections with friends, family, and colleagues. This may be a result of shared beliefs and values as well as an understanding and acceptance of others who have different purposes. Those reporting a lack of purpose in their lives reported increased feelings of loneliness and being more critical of others.

When I first read this list, I thought about my own life. When I was much younger, healthier, and working for someone else, I used most of my sick days each year. Since I started working for myself twenty-five years ago, I don't think I've taken fifty total sick days, including the fourteen days I was in bed with COVID-19, the seven days after tearing my Achilles, the five days I took off for back surgery, and another day or two here and there.

Why have I worked so hard, and where did I find the oxygen to keep going?

Think back to when you were excited about something new in your life.

- Did you get up early and stay up late thinking about it?
- Do you take on more responsibility for things you care more about or less about?
- When you really want something, how much more pushback can you handle?
- How do you feel when you meet someone new who has a passion for something you love?

Purpose and passion come from your heart, not your cranium. Purpose helps us prioritize, make decisions, push through adversity, and achieve more. The benefits don't stop there. As social beings, this sense of purpose helps us connect with others, which is an integral part of our survival!

MY MENTOR, FRIEND, AND BROTHER

Throughout my career in financial services, I met a lot of good people and a number of people I wish I hadn't met. I assume this is the case in most industries, but my observation is that there is a greater likelihood of finding selfish people in high-paying or highly competitive industries. My absolute favorite person in the financial, insurance, wealth management, and estate planning worlds is my friend Doug Hostetler. Ironically, Doug is a highly competitive man, having been recruited to play quarterback for Penn State under Joe Paterno in the mid to late 1970s.

What makes Doug such a happy person, a wonderful conversationalist, and a gifted advisor and mentor is his patience. This patience comes from his clear understanding of his purpose in life. In his words, Doug's faith-based purpose is "To know Him and to let Him be known." You don't have to be religious (in fact, I'm a recovering Catholic who does not attend any church) to appreciate that Doug looks for signs of God in everyone he meets and in every situation. His patience, curiosity, and open-mindedness are still a marvel to me after decades of working together and being friends. If you like this book, you can thank Doug too. He was a significant influence in getting me to put other things aside and follow my purpose with this book.

As I consider Doug and our giraffe friends, I have a simple but not easy question for you.

Have you been living and working from your head or from your heart?

When it comes to our eighteen-foot-tall role models, their heads are only a small part of their makeup. And without their big hearts pumping life throughout their bodies, they wouldn't last a second.

Our brains consume energy, lots of it. But our hearts deliver energy. Living from our heads is exhausting. Living from our hearts is energizing for us and for those in our tower.

MOMMA KNOWS BEST

My mother, Dorothy Fogarty, is the hardest-working and most thoughtful person I know. I'm not the only one who thinks that about her. For thirty years, she drove fifty miles each way to her job at Quality Beverage, the largest independent Anheuser-Busch distributor in the United States. The company's creed is to "Always do the 'right thing.'" Each year, they award one employee with the "Spirit of the Creed."

> WHY ARE GIRAFFES SLOW TO APOLOGIZE?
>
> BECAUSE IT TAKES THEM A LOOOOOONG TIME TO SWALLOW THEIR PRIDE.

Mom won the first award in 1997 and again in 2005 and 2010. In 2020, she was voted the award again, but they decided not to give her the award. Instead, Quality Beverage decided to rename the honor the "Dot Fogarty Spirit of the Creed Award." When your peers, bosses, customers, or direct reports honor you, it's because you did something for them that nobody else did. That's what it means to have a huge heart—and to follow it.

FOR BUSINESS

"Survival of the fittest," "Only the strong survive," and "Kill or be killed," were phrases initially used to describe animal behavior but were later adopted as descriptions of business. Movies such as *Swimming with the Sharks* and *Glengarry Glen Ross* further perpetuate the brutal reality.

This is the lion or tiger mentality, which is fine if you happen to be the largest, fastest, strongest apex predator in your space. What happens if you don't have the largest company with the best products and the best people? What happens if you don't have a winner-takes-all mentality and don't want to claw your way to the top (literally and figuratively)? This is where the giraffe can teach us a better way in business.

We live in a much different world today than the one which existed only one generation ago. Twenty years ago, news stories had to be in before the 6:00 p.m. news hour or submitted to the newspaper editor way before he went to press at 11:00 p.m. If you missed the deadline, the story would be pushed off to the next day or never published. But today, before some brute beast has a chance to retract an ill-considered selfie or Tweet, the news has traveled worldwide.

Sure, your business may have lots of good news to share, but we all know bad news travels much faster. Consumers benefit from this endless stream of information, but your business must navigate that stream every day. And you know what lives in those waters.

Perhaps you have heard the adage, "Nobody cares how much you know until they know how much you care." There is indisputable evidence that this is the case in all areas of business, not just in some cheesy sales seminar, which I may have attended—and given—more than a few times in my life.

The younger generations are impacting societal norms as well. Surveys show that millennials and the younger generation value quality of life and social causes much more than previous generations. Whether you want to avoid the negative backlash or you truly want to embrace the younger generation and its values, you must learn how to follow your huge heart, like the giraffe.

According to *Fast Company*'s survey in 2021 about an organization's stated purpose:

1. 78 percent of people were more likely to remember a company with a strong purpose.
2. 78 percent were more likely to want to work for that company.
3. 72 percent were more likely to forgive the company for a mistake.
4. 67 percent said they consider company purpose when deciding what to buy.[28]

I have worked with many boomers and Gen Xers who dismiss some of these statistics as being indicative of people without work experience, presuming that these sentimentalities will change as they mature. But what is the cost of being wrong in that assumption?

Consider these eye-opening, if not troubling, statistics that I found in a very interesting article in *Forbes* magazine:

1. By 2025, 75 percent of the workforce will be millennials, and they are looking for socially responsible employers.
2. 64 percent of millennials won't take a job if their employer doesn't have a strong Corporate Social Responsibility (CSR).

3. Purpose-driven companies had 40 percent higher
    levels of workforce retention.[29]

Perhaps millennials are unrealistic in their expectations in the work-place, and they will change jobs much more frequently than the older generations did. What will that mean to those of us who employ them? The cost of losing an employee ranges from tens of thousands of dollars to 1.5-2.0 times an employee's annual salary. The total cost of employee turnover within US companies is estimated at $1 trillion annually![30]

Given that Coldwell Banker estimates that $68 trillion in wealth will be passed down from boomers to millennials and Generation Z over the next thirty years, it's hard to ignore the importance of reaching the next generation.[31]

Be the Giraffe is my seventeenth book. I confess that the first twelve books were written for one purpose—to generate clients for my financial firms. Though they successfully helped us grow our businesses, only one of those books sold a substantial number.

Conversely, the last four books were written with the sole motivation of helping people eliminate financial stress, get a handle on their life's purpose, and grow their businesses. These books have had much greater success. I don't think it's a coincidence.

Zig Ziglar said, "You can have everything you want in life if you will just help enough other people get what they want."[32] In 2019, Midland National Insurance Company hired me to teach a two-day Million Dollar Advisor Boot Camp, and I had an opportunity to put Zig's words to the test. We had a wonderful group of financial professionals contribute to a very productive event. At the end, I asked attendees what they got out of it. One gentleman, Scott, said that he was committed to taking control of his physical and emotional health and would take up his wood-burning hobby again. I asked him when he would start. He replied, "I will complete my next piece by Sunday (it was Friday). I was so happy to receive these two pictures in my email on Monday morning:

On Friday, I received a package. This generous expression of the heart made me want to teach more and opened my mind to writing this book.

The giraffe's enormous heart is the reason it can support that long neck. And that amazing neck supports the head that allows it to see things others can't and to reach things others won't. "People don't care how much you know until they know how much you care." Why? The difference is heart.

Standing out and reaching higher requires you to be in touch with what matters most to you so you can figure out what is more important to those around you.

Think of a particular interaction that touched your heart. Go ahead, I'll wait.

I bet the memory can be characterized by the generosity of the soul. Remember, the heart lives by giving it all away. And the more life it sends to other parts of the body, the more that comes back to it.

Ask yourself: What's one area of your life that's starved for oxygen?

Here's the giraffe-y view of the answer: Which one person do you know who needs some heartfelt kindness and generosity?

You know what to do. It's gonna make someone's day, and make your day too. Put this book down, please, and do it now.

CHAPTER 10
FEED DIFFERENTLY

THERE'S STUPIDITY IN NUMBERS. ASK AROUND.—CHRIS JARVIS

What can giraffes teach us about building better, stronger, more unique relationships?

You already know that billions of African herbivores eat grass. They follow the rains, decimate the terrain, and constantly migrate to greener pastures. They must keep moving because the grazed plains look more like the aftermath of a Burning Man event. And, as we discussed in Chapter 3, just like Burning Man, they will be back again next year to do it all again. The resulting dust from hungry herds announcing their approach or their departure signals this movable feast to predators.

Whether their heads are in the weeds eating grass or at shoulder height staring at the ass in front of them, migrators are unaware of what's truly happening around them. None of them voted on the plan to cross crocodile-infested waters or were part of a focus group deciding where to cross. One foal jumps in and everyone follows. There's stupidity in numbers.

I suppose giraffes could eat grass, like they could probably swim, but wisely choose the pristine leaves of trees. They can consume up to seventy-five pounds of leaves and twigs daily, so they are just as busy munching as the herd. The favorite tree of the giraffe is the acacia and this flora-fauna relationship is the most magical since Jack and the Beanstalk.[33]

The acacia has developed a couple of clever defenses to keep from being munched down to the trunk. First, the name acacia comes from the Greek word for thorns, and acacia, by any other name, would be just as painful. These thorns can be three inches long and as sharp as a needle. The giraffe counters with its dexterous eighteen-inch tongue and very tough lips, allowing it to work around the thorns to get at the tasty leaves.

Acacia's next move? Tannins. Yes, we as humans love our tannins, the water-soluble carbon-based compounds found in certain plants. We use them for food processing, leathermaking, and in wine and cocoa. They are not, however, kind to giraffes. They interfere with digestive enzymes and are very disruptive. For my Californian amigos, think about a Tijuana bacon-wrapped hot dog. For the New Yorkers and tri-staters, substitute White Castle, or four New York System hot wieners "all the way." In all cases, your decision starts out tasting great but always ends really badly.

When the giraffe works hard at the tree, stripping bits of the bark, the tannins are released into the air. As they reach different branches, the rest of the tree releases more tannins. The entire tree becomes bitter-tasting

(Leaf me alone!), and the giraffe moves on, leaving plenty on the buffet for others and sparing the life of the tree.

This dance continues in an even more fascinating way. The tannins released into the air will ride the wind, reaching trees up to fifty feet away. This causes those neighboring acacias to release their tannins and also become bitter. As a result, the giraffes learn to move upwind to approach trees that have not been embittered. This has a secondary benefit for the giraffe. Moving into the wind means the giraffes keep going away from their scent trail instead of walking into an area where their presence has already been announced, making them less likely to encounter predators. We know giraffes are smart, but I never said they don't stink a little.

> WHY DO GIRAFFES SING IN THE RAIN?
>
> BECAUSE THEY CAN'T FIT IN THE SHOWER.

This unique relationship between the acacia tree and the giraffe keeps giraffes from overgrazing, which is obviously good for the acacia tree but is also good for the species, as it saves food for other giraffes. This relationship also protects the giraffe by keeping it moving in the best direction for the giraffe!

When there is no path of environmental destruction and giraffes aren't in herds, predators can't find clues as to where all the giraffes are located. This symbiotic relationship between the giraffe and the tree is good for all giraffes and good for all the trees.

FOR YOU

The acacia tree and giraffe have a complex, interesting, and mutually beneficial relationship. There are many different micro lessons here for our everyday lives.

First, we must learn to be adaptable. Humans are social creatures. The good news is that there are over seven billion people on the planet, so you shouldn't have much trouble finding a few. Undoubtedly, there will be some people whose company you would like more of and others with whom you could use less. Let's think of leaves and thorns as these two categories of people.

Whether you see the person in question as the tasty leaves of the acacia tree or the sharp thorns, everyone benefits when we're curious. Instead of seeing the leaves and being surprised by thorns, or seeing the thorns and assuming the leaves aren't worth it, we should approach the situation like a giraffe.

The giraffe learned how to navigate the thorns to get to the leaves. This came from observation and careful exploration. Couldn't we all benefit from being a little more curious about others, rather than judgmental? What do you think would happen if we were a little more careful about how we interact with others? If we could pause to observe what people are thinking or feeling, instead of mindlessly acting on our needs, we might be able to save ourselves and others a lot of time and discomfort.

Second, you might say that eating acacia leaves requires patience. If giraffes ran away from an acacia tree every time they got needled, their population would be exactly zero today. Evolution is the ultimate adaptation of a species, and evolution takes time.

Third, the tannins of the acacia tree leave hints too. What does the giraffe do when its pleasant dining experience is interrupted by the change in circumstance? When the leaves become bitter, the giraffe accepts the change and moves forward. Sure, like when Neanderthals were forced to get up from their rocker to change the TV channel, it's inconvenient. The bitter leaves might become slightly unpleasant, but this change is good for the giraffe, even if it appears frustrating at the time.

When circumstances change for other people, and subsequently for our interactions with them, we could benefit by being more giraffe-like. Accept that there is change and move forward. It's very possible that what seems to be a major inconvenience or disruption is happening for a really good reason, even if we can't see it, and may not see it for a while.

During my interview with Owen Sammarone, creator of Unleash the Knowledge, he asked me what failures or setbacks would I try to "undo" if I could go back in time and be his age again. For background, he was twenty-four and I was fifty at the time. God knows I would love to avoid any unnecessary pain or anxiety, but the lessons learned from these experiences might have been worth it.

WHO MOVED MY LEAVES?

1. I was rejected from MBA programs that were ranked higher than UCLA. While there, I realized there was an entrepreneur inside me dying to get out. UCLA had the best entrepreneurship program of the schools on my application list.

2. I was kicked out of a company I started. It cost me millions of dollars and set me back years, but it gave me the opportunity to work with entrepreneurs and wealthy families, where I learned so many valuable lessons and made invaluable contacts. I haven't wished for one minute in the last fifteen years to be back in the old company or anything like it.

3. Like many people, I experienced a painful divorce. At the time, I thought I might never date anyone seriously again. I have been happily married for twelve years, have successfully navigated a blended family scenario, and have a good relationship with my ex-wife and her new family as well.

4. After I sold my company, the acquirers fired me and threatened not to pay me the millions of dollars in deferred payments they owed me. After four years in federal court and over $700,000 in legal fees, I was finally awarded some of what they owed me. More importantly, the drawn-out legal battle gave me time to explore other options.

THE LONGEST LESSON OF MY LIFE

Matt and I met in freshman English class at Classical High School. We played baseball and basketball together all four years. He was voted funniest guy in our school, deservedly so. Though I moved 2,500 miles away, I would still see Matt and other high school friends when visiting family. Decades later, it was heartbreaking to hear that he was diagnosed with multiple myeloma, an incurable form of cancer that attacks the blood and the bones. I was back in Rhode Island for my twenty-year college reunion and planned to see Matt before the festivities. When I ran into a bunch of classmates at the airport, I asked Matt if a longer visit Sunday would be better than a shorter visit on Friday. He agreed and told me to go and have fun.

On Sunday morning, I called Matt to let him know I was on my way. His wife Kim answered and told me Matt had had a rough night and had finally got to sleep. I could come over, but he likely wouldn't wake up. I didn't want to watch Matt sleep, I wanted to hang out, so I told Kim I would see him in eleven days when I came back to Rhode Island.

Matt passed away that Friday. For eight years, I carried that event as my biggest regret in life. I hated myself for not making a visit with my sick friend the top priority.

Fast-forward to 2020, my father had been fighting multiple myeloma for seven years. He needed to be hospitalized just after the COVID-19 pandemic hit. Thankfully, he was discharged, but his prospects were scary. Dad lived alone in a condo building with exposure to hundreds of people and he was getting out of the hospital with no idea what kind of risks he was facing.

I called one of my clients and asked if I could rent his jet. For $21,000, the price of the pilot and fuel, I could pick up my father and bring him home with me. I'd never spent more than $2,000 on a plane ticket, but I couldn't risk it. My dad was very weak for the first few days, then began to recover.

We had a wonderful week with him before he showed some signs of delusion. Was it possibly dementia or just a side effect of all his meds?

I brought him to the hospital for blood work. They sedated him, and he never woke up. If I had not carried the pain and self-hatred over Matt, I don't know if I would have spent $21,000 to bring my dad home. I wouldn't have spent that last ten days with him, which I had no idea would be his last ten. My greatest regret in life gave me my greatest gift. You just don't know what you have sometimes.

Can you think of a time in your life when you had something happen that seemed awful at the time but ended up being a blessing?

Here's a hint from the giraffe: Every bitter change or thorny exchange can turn out for your good.

Fourth and finally, the giraffe-acacia soap opera teaches us about the importance of timing in any relationship. The leaves are sweet but hard to reach. Once you interact with them, your behavior that was tolerated at first is now the irritant that makes the leaves bitter. If you are the giraffe, you may think that continuing to eat until the tree sees how important it is for you to be correct is the right move. But, you will eventually learn that the harder you try to make the situation change, the more bitter the tree gets toward you. If you leave the tree alone for a while, the bitterness wears off, and the leaves become sweet again.

(For giraffe-y reasons, the author has been advised by his agent not to offer any marriage stories to illustrate this point.)

Does this sound like any, or every, relationship you have had?

FOR BUSINESS

At first glance, the acacia tree may seem to tease the giraffe with its tasty leaves, only to become bitter and shun the giraffe. But upon closer inspection, you see that the little dance between the acacia tree and the giraffe and the other acacia trees and the other giraffes is a thing of beauty. All the seemingly competing parties benefit from this give-and-take. Maybe you have heard the phrase, "Nature always finds a way." In what might be my favorite lesson of the book, that is certainly the case as "feeding" differently is such an important lesson for any business.

Why? Because there are so many inherent conflicts of interest in any commercial enterprise. Consider the following areas where businesses must strike a delicate balance for mutual benefit:

On One Hand	On The Other
Employees want higher pay	Payroll reduces profitability
Employees want great benefits	Benefits cut into earnings
Customers want high-quality products	Product innovation is expensive
Customers want great service	Service departments are costly
Customers want lower prices	Lower margins require greater efficiencies
Employees want more time off	Employers need employees to work harder
Vendors want to sell more product	Employers want to carry less overhead

There is nothing wrong with either party for wanting what they want. As frustrating as this juggling act can be, it gives you the opportunity to create more giraffe-y relationships with the other stakeholders.

In fact, there are multiple applications of this lesson. We should start by thinking about what your company feeds from to survive in the short term and what your company really needs to thrive over the longer term.

9 Key Factors that Fuel Business Growth

- Energizing Leadership
- Clear Strategy
- Creative Financing
- Marketing & Sales
- Personnel Development
- Proprietary Technology
- Quality Control
- Innovation / Research & Development
- Culture

A major problem in any one of the above areas could sink your company. However, if you want to have a successful business, you don't need to master all of these. You may only need to be extraordinary in a couple of areas, or the absolute best in your industry in one, to stand out and rise above the herd of competition.

You may have someone at the top of your organization who is so intelligent, innovative, or inspirational that people are willing to run through walls to take the company to the next level. Steve Jobs at Apple, Howard Schultz at Starbucks, Elon Musk at Tesla, and Jeff Bezos at Amazon are pretty good examples.

Culture and personnel are the backbone of companies like Nordstrom and Ritz-Carlton. For both organizations, employees are empowered and expected to solve problems on the spot. I have had Nordstrom workers drop off my tailoring at my home after hours so I could have my tux in time to board a plane for a formal event in another country.

Perhaps you've had the pleasure of staying at a Ritz-Carlton. If you have, and you had some type of problem with your room, your meal, or your delivery to the business center, you may have noticed something different. The first person you talked to about your problem was the last. That person will not leave you until the problem is solved. As a result, many people are willing to pay more for these two brands because they value extraordinary service.

When you think about your company, with which group of people do you have a uniquely positive relationship? Do you have an extraordinary relationship with your salespeople or distributors? Do you pay them more or support them considerably better than your competitors do? What do you do for your customers that nobody else in your industry does?

USAA sells a commodity product, insurance. To every other company, they have "policyholders" or "insureds." Not at USAA—they call their customers "members." Their 2019 ad campaign features customers claiming to be members for life. Does this work? Hell yes it does. In my experience, the average retention of a property casualty insurance company is about 80 percent. The niche market of military families is their acacia tree, and they enjoy an outrageous retention rate of 96 percent. For you more advanced data giraffes, USAA has the highest Net Promoter Scores in home insurance, auto insurance, and banking for eleven straight years.[34]

If you don't know where your acacia tree is, think about where you can go for help. Yes, there are a great many business consultants, but you don't need a consultant yet! What you need to do first is ask the people who know the most about you right now.

Ask your customers questions you're afraid to ask. I promise you'll wonder what took you so long.

Ask your team questions that make you feel vulnerable. That's half the challenge. The next half is following up on what you hear.

My first financial company provided financial planning, insurance, and investment services to physicians. We had a specialty knowledge of asset protection, which was a hot area at the time with many states suffering from medical malpractice crises. Helping physicians protect their wealth against lawsuits brought us a lot of attention, but the bulk of our income came from investment management fees and insurance commissions. At the time, there were over one million licensed financial professionals who could have sold any of our clients the exact same products we did. So we developed a wonderful marketing strategy to stand out in a specific niche.

We wrote several financial books for doctors and a Continuing Medical Education (CME) monograph (specialty publication) that any specialist in any state could use to satisfy annual licensing requirements. We then leveraged the credibility we earned from those publishing credentials to publish over 200 articles in fifty different medical journals and to speak at over 200 hospitals and medical society meetings. Our specialization in one niche, and our unique knowledge about asset protection led over 15,000 doctors to contact us.

In the competitive business landscape, you could try to please and attract business from everyone, to be grasses for the masses, or you could be the acacia tree—thorny and out-of-reach for some, and that's the point.

Another challenge with targeting the masses is what I like to call the "Walmart effect." The only tried and true strategy for reaching outrageous numbers of customers is to be the low-cost provider. It's an easy idea to grasp: We all would rather pay $9 than $10 for the same item. The problem is, it's the most dangerous business model. This approach to gain clients will end up being a "race to zero" profit.

Focusing on feeding the masses will eat your company alive. When you're spread too thin, the masses will come, trample what's left of you, and move on to the next. Your business will look like the aftermath of Burning Man, and you'll be the one who ends up burnt-out.

Giraffes will appreciate your unique position and visit you regularly, but not too often. Acacia trees are honest about who they are. They tell their customers about their limitations, and politely ask them to take a hike occasionally.

Giraffes and acacia trees have one of the most interesting relationships in the natural world. Their complicated, symbiotic relationship is a great model for anyone or  any organization that deals with people.

Who do you or your business "feed" from, and who "feeds" from you? There are a lot of lessons about win-win relationships from the giraffe-acacia love fest, so let's recap.

Be adaptable. Don't quit when you encounter some thorns.

Be curious. Ask questions, especially ones that scare you.

Be careful and be patient. Timing is everything, but not everyone is on your timeline.

Be weird. (Sounds nicer than "exclusive," but that's really my point.)

In your personal or business relationships, which one of these attributes do you need to work on today? Surprise! I have a recommendation.

Who do you need to ask scary questions about yourself or your business? You know, like, "What's an area I can improve on as your partner?" Or, "What do you like the least about doing business with us?"

You might get an earful of thorns, but look for the leaves.

CHAPTER 11

SURVIVE THE DROP

I LOVE BIRTHDAY SURPRISES.
EXCEPT FOR THE ONE I HAD ON
MY ACTUAL BIRTH DAY.
—BABY GIRAFFE

What do giraffes learn on day one that the rest of us desperately need to know about life?

Imagine yourself as a baby giraffe, before it's born. You will have more than enough time to get comfortable with this idea because, usually, the larger the animal, the longer the pregnancy. A typical giraffe's gestation period is fifteen months, about 50 percent longer than a human's. Consider that a baby giraffe can be over six feet tall and almost 150 pounds at birth, approximately my size in seventh grade. It makes sense that the bun needs a bit more time in the oven.[35]

Many mothers have told me that they forgot (or blocked out) the painful aspects of childbirth; otherwise, they would have never consider the outrageous idea of having another. This is nature's way of ensuring the survival of the species. Speaking from personal experience with physical discomfort, I nearly jumped off the doctor's table when he gave me an epidural for my neuropathy after a complicated Achilles tendon repair. Since I found the remedy to birthing pain to be awful, I will give the ladies a clear win in the category of dealing with pain. But I digress.

Yes, childbirth is hard on the mother. But since this book is about changing our perspective and seeing things differently, let's try to think about childbirth from the baby giraffe's perspective. Imagine sleeping in a warm, dark, cozy bed. Add to the image of that comfort the fact that you don't have to get out of bed to eat or to go to the bathroom. In utero, all of that is taken care of for you, so you're never hungry, cold, or uncomfortable. This is the giraffe's existence for fifteen months. Until it isn't.

After a tumultuous labor that may last as little as thirty to sixty minutes, the giraffe is born. To put that conception-to-exit timeline into perspective, that is the equivalent of sleeping for eight hours, then being awoken and yanked out of bed in three seconds. That is certainly a bit abrupt. But wait! It gets even better—or worse if you love your snooze button.

What could make it even more disruptive for a baby giraffe? Yup. You guessed it. Giraffes are so committed to maintaining their elevated perspective that they don't just eat standing up. They also give birth while standing. Perhaps this is to preserve its perch to keep an eye out for predators. I completely understand that self-preservation is a strong instinct, but what about this newborn's preservation?

Before the baby giraffe can adjust its eyes to its first glimpse of the blinding sunlight, it gets to experience one of the three fears humans possess at birth. A newborn giraffe gets to experience the fear and reality of falling, as it drops over six feet to the ground. Motion sickness, blinding light, chills, helpless falling, and an abrupt jolt as they get their first taste of gravity—these are all experienced within the first minutes of a giraffe's life on terra firma. Welcome!

Despite the trauma, they fight to stand, wobbling and falling until they find their balance. This is even more amazing when you consider they've never had to hold up those long necks! The first few steps are awkward and uncomfortable. After all, those legs have been folded up in utero for fifteen months. I lose feeling in my legs if I'm scrolling through my phone in the bathroom for fifteen minutes.

As crazy as it all sounds, this is how countless millions of giraffes have started their lives over the last twenty-five million years. They survived the drop—and you will, too.

FOR YOU

From giraffes, we can learn so much about change. From the mother's standpoint, they see that there is an abrupt change in store for their child, yet there is nothing they can do but provide a supportive environment for them when they go through it. This has lots of applications in parenting, friendship, and relationships.

We also see that change can be difficult. And as disturbing and startling as it might seem at the time, there isn't a lot of value in revisiting why this change happened. The baby giraffe doesn't try to understand physics or biology, nor does it take issue with its mother for putting it through such a harrowing experience. The giraffe immediately accepts its situation, does its best to stand up, and tries to take its first steps. Within minutes, the giraffe is walking. In less than an hour, it could be running. It develops a strong bond with its mother, builds social connections, and begins a very different life.

Giraffe childbirth illustrates how change can be difficult, abrupt, and outside of our control. The giraffe teaches us that change isn't the end of the world, even if the change is untimely, unexpected, uncomfortable, or even traumatic.

Think about the worst things that have happened in your life. Think about the worst things that have happened to people around you.

You survived. Congratulations.

My pal, Art Markman, is the vice provost of the University of Texas-Austin and a bestselling author with a popular podcast. He is also a professor of neuroscience with an impressive teaching and administrative track record. I recall one of his lectures when he was talking about the human being's ability to survive trauma. He said people severely overestimate the impact that events will have on our lives. He brought up the "set point" philosophy which states that people go back to their normal levels of happiness even after the most amazing or most horrible situations. Miserable people who win the lottery go back to being miserable. Happy people may suffer the death of loved ones or misfortune, but they will eventually go back to being happy people. It doesn't mean that they ever forget these events. It just means that people do find their way back to their normal emotional levels.

Can you recall a time in your life when you were devastated by an event? Perhaps it was a breakup, loss of a job, bad investment outcome, physical injury, or a failed business.

Throughout this book, I have attempted to lead by example, sharing many of the challenging times in my life. The list below includes many of the stories I've already shared and some that are used in other books or articles:

1. Rejected by Duke University
2. Injured my shoulder/end of baseball career
3. Failed marriage
4. Rejected by Stanford, Kellogg, Wharton
5. Younger sister/father/friend/biz partner passed away
6. Kicked out of a company I started
7. Lost millions of dollars (leaving me with $0)
8. Failed businesses
9. Countless others I may have forgotten or blocked out

For each of these events, I can look back and see that the pain I felt was temporary. I now have great memories of people who are no longer in my life and a great appreciation for the lessons I learned from the chapters that have closed.

In your experience, did you find it very helpful to be constantly sharing, rehashing, or complaining about the event? Alternatively, did you find that when you were busy with something else, you were able to take your mind off the negative event and focus on something else?

I just watched the Arnold Schwarzenegger documentary on Netflix. His taskmaster father taught him to "stay busy … and be useful." When asked if he was depressed when his brother and father passed away, he responded, "Depression is something I never had time for because I was too busy."[36]

The baby giraffe has no time for therapy, it must stand up, get on its feet, and get moving.

My friend Ana Rubio, a physical education teacher and founder of Streamline Miami, taught me a lot about survival—and thrival! When she got fed up with losing her students to gangs and gang violence, she decided to do something about it. She didn't get city funding for her non-profit, an organization sorely needed to help her inner-city kids. She didn't get much support from her student's parents either. Still, she took it upon herself to help the kids attending her school and other schools in the area. She campaigned for resources and built a relationship with the University of Miami. She travelled around the country speaking out for people to help their teachers and their schools. She stood up and got busy being useful. In six years, the school she served went from a "D" rating to an "A." How did they do it? Ana took it upon herself and never stopped moving forward, even when she heard a chorus of Nos and a symphony of "You can't do that by yourself." She rallied other teachers, administrators, and even my wife and me (from 1,200 miles away) to help her.

> **This is a very quick and easy exercise that should make a point rather quickly.**
>
> **Take your two hands and put them together so you alternate your fingers. This is called clasping your hands. When you look down, the top thumb will be either your left or your right.**
>
> **If your top thumb is your right thumb, the next finger**

will be your left thumb, then the right index, then the left index, etc.

If you look down and your top thumb is your left thumb, then your right thumb, left index finger, right index finger, etc..

That probably feels pretty comfortable.

Now, take the bottom hand and move it so that it's the top hand. If you previously started with the left thumb on top, make your right thumb on top. Then alternate so as to put your hands the way they were before. If you previously started with your right thumb on top, put your left thumb on top. And alternate.

How does that feel?

If you are like 95 percent of my seminar attendees, it probably felt pretty awkward or uncomfortable. In a live seminar, I will often see people shake out their hands and go back to how they started.

This exercise shows you that anytime we do something different, even something that shouldn't be really all that different, it feels off, odd, awkward, and wrong. The natural tendency is to go back to something we are more familiar with doing.

When you make a change in your life, you will likely feel uncomfortable. If you typically get up at 6:30 a.m. to get ready for work, you can imagine that adding a health routine that has you getting up at 5:00 a.m. to go to the gym will be a little uncomfortable. If you are working on your finances and trying to save money, you may have to tell someone "No" when asked to go out. This won't be easy at first, but you will survive.

Learn to be comfortable with being uncomfortable. You must do this, or you will have to learn how to be happy with what you have and never want more.

FOR BUSINESS

My go-to quote as an undergraduate in the Sigma Phi Epsilon fraternity was, "The whole is greater than the sum of its parts." I have carried this quote to every culture, community, and nonprofit event. It means that together, we can do more than we can as a collection of individuals.

When you apply this chapter's giraffe lesson to your company, you must first understand that your company is made up of individuals and you sell to individuals. Even if you have a business-to-business (B2B) offering, there is an individual in that organization deciding to work with you. What you need to appreciate is that these people will be dealing with changes, and they will present you with changes.

As a giraffe, you will stand out, and people will look up to you. Leading by example is the most powerful message you can send, and your actions will attract people who act, or want to act, the way that you do. If a leader focuses on placing the blame on others, he will build an organization of "blamers." If you look for the positive in every situation, you will attract people who want to look at things differently. Zebra and wildebeest multiply. Hyenas call for more hyenas. Giraffes attract more giraffes.

You may be familiar with the phrase "An ounce of prevention is worth a pound of cure," or, as I say in any other country, "A gram of prevention is worth a kilo of cure." Being a giraffe will help you

> **WHAT DO GIRAFFES HAVE THAT NO OTHER ANIMAL HAS?**
>
> **BABY GIRAFFES!**

see many changes approaching and give you time to prepare. But no matter how much you plan, your business will still be forced to deal with abrupt and involuntary changes that come not only from your personnel but also from your industry, competitors, regulations, technology, and the economy.

If you are running a public company, you are aware of how small things can have a significant effect on your stock price. It makes sense that you could fall short of an analyst's anticipated income numbers and see your stock price drop. What's crazy is that you could meet or outperform estimates and still suffer. I had a client in the technology space explain that a smaller company could outperform its expected earnings, but if two of the industry leaders reported lower-than-expected earnings, the entire sector could see a drop in stock price.

In a smaller company or professional practice, this is an even greater challenge. You may not have investors, but you likely have very limited resources. If you had lots of money and lots of people, you wouldn't be small. As a small company, you can't just issue new stock and generate years of operating expenses. You must make payroll, pay rent, and pay your suppliers. What happens if one of your biggest clients is treating your staff poorly? You don't want the negative energy. You want your staff to respect you as someone who protects and respects them. What if you can't afford to not have the client's revenue right now? What do you do?

You're gonna do the right thing. And if there's a drop in revenue you'll survive.

You will have to initiate some big changes in your company. These will not be abrupt to you since you're the one making the decisions. But your choices could be rather abrupt and disruptive to your employees, customers, vendors, or partners.

During my decade in Vistage, most of the tough decisions our chapter members made were very unpopular and extremely uncomfortable for at least one person. In some cases, the decisions were unpopular and uncomfortable for everyone. One of the most common lessons that we learned over time was that the fear of the decision was much worse than any blowback or repercussions that the decision caused.

There was not a single event, of the hundreds of events we discussed in the group, where we looked back and wished we had waited a little longer to break bad news, fire someone, or discontinue a strategic relationship.

Even the baby giraffe teaches us to look to the future and to pick our heads up when we have an unexpected fall. With the right attitude and a commitment to taking a determined step forward in some direction, we can move toward a better outcome, even after the most startling situations.

BE THE CHANGE

The changes needed to become a giraffe will seem abrupt, startling, and scary. When you start something new, there will not be comfort or guarantees. But you will survive. Others have risked everything to chase their dream and failed, then succeeded. FEAR is merely Fantasized Experiences Appearing Real. Don't let fear hold you back. Look in the mirror and channel Gloria Gaynor—I will survive!

The giraffe has no idea how to stand or walk, but it sure does try. It takes this action in the absence of surety. Call it Faith. Faith is, "the assurance of things hoped for, the conviction of things not seen."[37] When you are doing something big, you have no other choice than to give your heart to it. Pouring your heart into something can make the endeavor even scarier.

But consider this. The guaranteed outcomes from not changing and not trying are regret, failure, and everything else you think you're afraid of. How's that for a motivational meme?

Several years ago, I was at an industry conference at the Four Seasons in Las Colinas, Texas. I ran into an old friend, Tim Olson, a Regional Vice President for a whale of a company. Think about insurance company logos, you'll get it. He asked me how I was doing. At that time, I was pretty unhappy with my life, and I didn't sugarcoat how unhappy I was in the financial services industry. His giraffe-y response?

"I think you like it just the way it is, Chris. I know this because you're a brilliant and resourceful guy. If you wanted it to be different, you would change it."

Those words dropped me.

My water buffalo response? "Fuck you, Tim Olson!" Who the hell are you to tell me what I want? I don't even know what I want, how can you?"

Okay, I was thinking that, while chuckling and mumbling something about nothing.

As I was figuratively trying to stand up, I realized Tim was right.

I took the scary steps necessary to sell my company, changed the way I worked so I didn't need infrastructure, and started focusing on writing, teaching, and speaking.

Thanks again, Tim.

Drops happen.

Even if baby giraffe had a heads-up before its birth day, that innocent creature wouldn't understand what was about to happen, let alone be able to do anything to prevent or prepare for it. That's how many drops in life happen, of course. Don't worry about those. Worry just makes things worse.

If you hang around giraffes who want the best for you, you'll have the pleasure of some tough-but-true words from your tower. Pay attention to those. Their wisdom can sometimes make the difference between death and life.

But for this moment, I invite you to focus on another type of "drop"—the ones you initiate. Maybe we should call them leaps. Leaps of faith.

There's no guarantee you'll land in the best outcome. But I promise you can learn a lot if you keep trying and keep leaping, and you will eventually make it.

So, I will adapt some giraffese from my friend Tim for you to take into consideration.

I think you do not like things the way they've been. I know this because you're intelligent and resourceful. You want to be different and are ready to change!

What big change will you start today?

Don't just decide to change, but ask what action you will take to make the dominoes start falling.

CHAPTER 12

STRUT YOUR (STRANGE) STUFF

I WAS SELF-CONSCIOUS ABOUT
MY HEIGHT TILL I MET LARRY BIRD.
—CHRIS JARVIS

What can giraffes teach us about the dangers of trying to fit in?

What do you notice when you look at a giraffe? Of course, you will notice how tall they are. At eighteen feet, there is no animal close to their height. Next, you may notice the length of a giraffe's neck. At six feet in length, their neck alone is longer than most people are tall. Perhaps you're mesmerized by the maze-like pattern of their fur. Another unique characteristic of giraffes is that their fur patterns are like human fingerprints; no two are the same.

Back in Chapter 3, you learned from the giraffe that balance is B.S. What's less obvious until someone points it out is that a giraffe's body is far from symmetrical. Its front legs are 10 percent longer than its back legs. As a result, the giraffe's body is tilted back slightly. This is completely different from a horse or cow, whose torsos are basically parallel to the ground. The giraffe's unique design allows it to stand up straight (kinda) and support its heavy neck and head without toppling over.

You may also notice that a giraffe's legs are long, and their body is relatively short. I only noticed this because it's the exact opposite of my body. I'm 6'3" and only have a 31-inch inseam. I'm all torso, making me very tall in wheelchair basketball and making headroom the most important part of any new car search.

The giraffe's disproportionate weight distribution and shorter body give it an unusual gait. When most antelope walk, the front and back legs alternate. This means that the back left leg will move at the same time as the front right leg. The back legs move into the footprints of the front legs. The giraffe—and the camel—walk differently.

Giraffes and camels do what's called pacing or ambling. There are a couple explanations for this unique gait. Giraffes and camels both have long legs, short bodies, and big feet. By lifting both legs on the same side of the body at the same time, they prevent the fore and hind feet from getting in each other's way. Another explanation is that this method of walking is used to conserve energy. Given the massive size of the giraffe and the desert environment of the camel, the need to conserve energy passes the smell test.

This funky gait, which I may go so far as to call a strut, is reminiscent of a runway model with attitude or scenes from my freshman-year go-to movie, *Saturday Night Fever*. To age myself, we used to watch it on my roommate Joe Corrente's laser disk player. How can you not take notice of such a thing? When giraffes walk around with this regal don't-give-a-shit attitude, it must make even the most attentive predators tilt their heads. Predators instinctively look for members of the herd that stand out as injured or weak. For some reason, few lion prides have mastered hunting giraffes. Perhaps this full-time "Humpty Dance" throws them for a loop and keeps giraffes off the menu. It's so hard for lions to identify the differences are between strong and weak giraffes since they all look like they are broken.

Creating confusion is an effective survival technique and uniqueness is the most valuable mating strategy. Both work for our friend, Mr. G. Raffe.

FOR YOU

Giraffes teach us that even when we have lots of things in common, like all mammals do, small differences can change how people look at us, what we do, and how we do it.

In 2018, two years before the COVID-19 pandemic, the health insurer Cigna reported that 46 percent of Americans reported feeling loneliness and 43 percent reported feeling isolated. More troublingly, the same report shared that only 27 percent felt they belonged to a group of friends. Unsurprisingly, Millennials and Gen Z reported much more worrisome numbers than older generations.

As I write this, my three kids are 15–21 years of age. I can remember how upset they were when they found out that they had different lunch periods than many of their friends. The fear of missing out on that social interaction was a big deal. Even as an adult, and one who teaches mindfulness, I feel some pressure not to miss out on social gatherings with our friends.

The giraffe teaches us several valuable lessons in individuality. They aren't comfortable bending over to eat grass with the group, so they eat leaves from tall trees. This difference imparts so many benefits if you consider being unique an advantage. I sure do. Few describe the giraffe's gait as graceful with their weirdly long neck and disproportionate legs causing their strange steps. A giraffe isn't a better zebra—it's a whole different animal, and it embraces those qualities.

An overarching theme of this book is that different is better than better. What makes us different is what makes any group more interesting, more creative, and more effective. The giraffe teaches us not to hide.

You are different. Show it off.

At the age of forty-six, I finally got back into shape and started playing basketball again. In my third game, I ruptured my Achilles tendon. I was devastated, knowing it would be a long and painful rehab. After my surgery, the nurse asked me what color cast I wanted, suggesting black, grey, and dark blue. You should have seen the look on her face when I said, "Let's go with hot pink."

"I love it, but why pink?" she asked. I replied that there are three reasons. First, I am going to be on a knee scooter, so there is no hiding the fact that I am hurt and in a cast. Second and third, the only people who will care about my cast color are my daughters, who were twelve and nine at the time, and they would love it!

I was wrong about the second rationale, but dozens commented on the color of my cast, saying things like, "How fun!" or "It takes a real man to wear pink." Incidentally, I wear pink or purple almost all the time, and I find that people respond very positively to fun, colorful displays.

Ezra Frech is a remarkable young man who was born without a fully formed hand. Later, doctors had to amputate his leg above the knee. I have been following his story because his father Clayton is one of my best friends. I was in Clayton and his wife Bahar's wedding years before Ezra was born.

Clayton, a competitive soccer player and avid surfer, understandably had some concerns that his son might not be able to enjoy sports and benefit from the lessons one can learn from competition, hard work, victory, and defeat. Fast-forward seventeen years and Ezra is a member of the U.S. Paralympics Track & Field team. He has competed in eleven countries and holds multiple national records. During the Golden State Warriors historic 2015–2016 season, they were attempting to set the record for most wins in an NBA season. At age eleven, Ezra was asked to give the pregame speech to the Warriors on the day they were to break that record.

When he was nine, he was a guest on *The Ellen DeGeneres Show* (December 9, 2014). When Ellen asked him if he had any advice for other kids, he responded, "Everyone is different. Whether you look different, you think different, or you act different. Mine happens to be I look different. And it's very obvious! But that doesn't mean that a

WHAT DO YOU CALL A GIRAFFE TRYING TO HIDE AMONG ZEBRAS?

TWISTED.

kid with four limbs doesn't have any challenges. Everybody has challeng-es and everybody stares at everybody. So you just got to know that being different is okay."

What have you been hiding about yourself, and why?

What is the best possible outcome that would result from you shar-ing the most unique experiences from your past or your seemingly un-usual desires for your future with some of the people who are closest to you?

FOR BUSINESS

When coaching start-ups about niche markets, elevator pitches, and de-veloping raving fans, we like to say, "If you try to be everything to every-body, you will end up meaning nothing to nobody." Poor grammar aside, the point is profound.

The giraffe teaches us not to hide but to proudly be ourselves. When you combine this with the lesson of being vulnerable and sticking your neck out, you learn to lift your head, enjoy what you are, and be okay with what you're not!

In the third lesson, we discussed how Apple abandoned product di-versification and a balanced product mix to focus on doing only three things. That wasn't the first time the company stuck its neck out. When Apple first came on the scene, they didn't try to take over IBM's market share. Instead, they went for a new market of computer users: students. Apple was able to upset the PC market in 1984 with the tagline, "The computer for the rest of us." And, "Soon, there will be two types of people. Those who use computers, and those who use Apples."

In 1999, at the height of the profits in the stock market with the growth of the dot com companies, E*TRADE ran a commercial with the tagline, "Be Your Own Sugar Daddy." They proudly claimed, "E*TRADE. The number one place to invest online." [38]

Those of you from the Jurassic period like I am might remember a soft drink with the slogan, "The un-cola."

You get the idea: Celebrate what makes you unique. But stay with me. I'm not interested in lame motivational quotes or boring platitudes. If you don't be the giraffe and take some scary steps, you will be both lame and boring.

Stay lame and boring, and your only companions will be vultures. I'm not trying to be cute. This is for real.

After meeting the famed business consultant Jay Abraham, I agreed to fund, or "executive produce," a film about his life. As an executive producer, I was given a free one-on-one meeting with Jay to discuss my business. He sent every producer the same 100-page questionnaire and offered to review it before the meeting, which I did. When I got to his office, he started off by apologizing because he didn't have time to review my intake form before the meeting. He went on to confirm my suspicion that no one had ever filled out the form before I did. He then had his assistant, Destiny, schedule another meeting with me to go over the form. Mission accomplished. I stood out and we had multiple discussions.

When I met Jack Canfield at an event to discuss the *Be the Giraffe* movement, I wore one of many shirts with images of a giraffe on it every day of the conference. Does branding work? On day six, we came back from a break. Jack said he was in the hotel gift shop and saw the stuffed animal (a giraffe). He asked the group, "How could I NOT buy it for my friend? Chris Jarvis, come up here."

When I had the opportunity to work with my first billionaire client, it could have been an intimidating experience. This family had over two hundred full-time employees in their family office. I had three employees. When they asked me how large my organization was, I told them it was small because what we did wasn't time-intensive. I said that we were successful because we were very creative in our up-front planning and then noted that, once the planning was done, the execution was relatively easy and straightforward. What my new client was paying for was the creativity, not the administration. If they wanted someone with lots of employees and overhead to handle mundane tasks, we were the wrong group to hire.

I was confident in what I offered, and he became confident in me. Only because I decided to do business differently and not try to blend into the herd was I able to be in the company of some other giraffes.

After a speech I gave to an audience of successful life insurance agents, a man introduced himself to me and then me to his father, Mike. The young agent offered to buy me a drink, which was funny because the event had an open bar and it was 9:30 a.m.

He proceeded to tell me the story of his father's return from the Korean War. He wanted to start a business but had no money. His solution was to apply for a loan, but he had no suit. Mike went to the tailor to buy a couple of nice suits and ties and shoes. When it came time to pay, he said to put it on credit. They said that he had no credit, to which he replied, "I just got done fighting for you in Korea. Give me some credit for that and some more credit for wanting to start a business."

They gave him credit for the clothes and the next morning he walked, because he had no car, to the bank at 8:45 a.m. The bank didn't open until 9:00 a.m. Mike walked up to the door with his briefcase in hand and a glimmer in his eye. He said good morning to the security guard who quickly opened the door for him and told him to have a good day. As he was standing in the middle of the bank, before it was open, a manager walked up to him and asked, "How can I help you?"

He replied, "I am here for a loan."

The manager responded, "We aren't open. How did you get in here?"

He said, "I walked up to the door, and the guard kindly opened it for me."

Skeptical of the tale, the manager yelled to the guard and asked, "Did you open the door for this man?"

"Yes, sir!" the guard replied.

"Why?" asked the manager.

"Because he works here. Look at him. He's at least a Vice President. I would have offered to carry his briefcase, too, but I had to watch the door," the guard responded.

Mike wasn't trying to convince the guard that he was someone else. This isn't a story about faking it until you make it. This is an example of how people see us the exact way that we see ourselves. Mike believed that he should have a loan. He believed that he should be in the bank early because he deserved to be treated specially. As a result, so did the guard. When Mike got the loan from the bank, it was ultimately because the banker believed in a man who believed in himself.

We all have hidden strengths that we shy away from using. And every person has weaknesses that they try to hide.

Both approaches are wrong and deadly. Yes, deadly to the life we truly want to enjoy.

What's one thing about yourself that you've been hiding or twisting?

What weakness can you turn into an advantage simply by sharing it with someone in your tower?

What do you want your employees, customers, investors, or community to think about you and about your company?

What do they need to see to demonstrate that you are different from your competition?

What do you need to think, believe, and do to demonstrate that you believe this?

CHAPTER 13

TASTE THE PEE

I'M OPEN TO NEW IDEAS, ESPECIALLY MY OWN.

Early in this book, I shared the story of my amazing safari in 2002 that became my motivation for this book. My father and my friend Lee Kaplan had a once-in-a-lifetime experience, spending twenty-four days, mainly in South Africa, Botswana, and Zimbabwe. On this bucket list trip to five different parks and game reserves, we took photographs of countless animals from dozens of species. One of the experiences that left a lasting impression on me involved giraffes. Shocker.

Sure, I've watched lots of nature shows, visited many zoos, and had several pets. I have even seen my share of animal mating. I wouldn't call myself a pervy Dr. Doolittle, but I've seen what I've seen, and it all looks pretty much the same. What surprised me on safari was when our guide stopped the Range Rover and whispered, "This giraffe wants to mate. You gotta see this!"

I thought giraffe mating might be interesting, in the same way watching someone walk a tightrope is interesting because of the unusual perspective of watching the spectacle. This wasn't what our guide was talking about.

As is the case with most mammals, male hormones drive the process. Without a place to take a long, cold shower, the male giraffe sets off to find a female in estrus. Giraffes are easy to spot, but the females have no outwardly visible sign of being in season, so nature created a different reason to lure the males and females closer to one another. Witnessing this in Botswana, I couldn't help but think back to my own lumbering approaches to single women back in Boston. In both cases, the females stood still and looked elsewhere, ignoring the curious male's attempts to interact.

As he approached each of the three females, he rubbed the side of his head against the female's buttocks. The female instinctively began to urinate.

The male then caught some of the urine on his tongue. Curling his lip, he triggers a flehmen response, which allows him to determine if the female is ovulating and ideally suited for breeding. Once the male notices that she is in estrus, the smooth-talking begins. This experience was a bit of a *Goldilocks and the Three Bears* scenario. The first female was too cold. The second female must have been too hot. The third was just right. I'll just leave the story right there.

Tasting the pee is the giraffe's unconventional key to continuing its species. What else would you expect?

FOR YOU

Abraham Lincoln famously tweeted, "I do not like that man. I need to get to know him better."

Male giraffes taste the pee of their potential partner as part of the successful continuation of their species. Could we call this an exercise in efficiency? Sure, but there's more we can learn. We don't have to like or trust every new idea or every person we encounter, but we'll do well to give each a little consideration.

Society progresses and ultimately finds success when we open our minds to new ideas, different people, and other cultures. I can be very opinionated, and this often takes the form of snap judgments and reactionary responses. In the case of stumbling across a king cobra, this can be a wonderful attribute, but it isn't always helpful when meeting new people or considering different paths.

Last weekend, my daughter invited me to a Spenga® class. I'm usually a fan of continuing education, but I soon realized this was an exercise class—an unholy mix of spinning, strength training, and yoga. Either she was trying to kill me, correctly assuming I have pretty good life insurance coverage, or she really enjoys spending time with me, especially when I'm trying new things.

I was so glad that I accepted her invitation. Now I know to never do that again! Lunch afterward was terrific, though.

Jack Canfield once told me, "The way you do something is the way you do everything." Either you approach life and the invitations it sends you with an open mind, or you don't. It's difficult to hover between the two postures. I learned that lesson well in Spenga®.

We learned that giraffe childbirth is a wonderful metaphor for dealing with the abrupt impact change can have on our lives. We learned that we need to get up and get moving first; maybe there will be time to complain or analyze the situation later. So far, we have focused on what to do. Here, we will think about how the baby giraffes successfully navigate the challenges of change.

Relatively speaking, giraffes have one of the largest births of mammals. A baby giraffe is one-tenth the size of its mother at the time of birth. Compare that to humans, who are born one-twenty-second the size of their mothers, elephants at one-twenty-sixth, and giant pandas who are tiny at one-nine hundredth. Giraffes do more growing in utero, meaning they need more parenting in the first days and weeks of life.

Doesn't this sound like the life of an innovator, visionary, entrepreneur, or giraffe? They need some encouragement, guidance, and reassurance so that they can go out and do great things.

Earlier in the book, I mentioned that I was raised Roman Catholic. In high school, I met, became friends with, and dated many Jewish classmates. However, it wasn't until I was forty-five years old that I attended my first bar mitzvah. My wife's best friend, Dana, invited us to her son Sammy's bar mitzvah in Westchester, New York. I can honestly say that it was the most moving religious experience I have ever attended.

In Catholicism, several of the sacraments that I participated in were group activities—namely holy penance, first communion, and confirmation. Multiple children of the parish completed the training together. In Judaism, the bar mitzvah and bat mitzvah are individual events. A teenager, about to enter a very confusing and difficult stage of life, is surrounded by his or her family, friends, and religious leaders to welcome him or her as a member of the Jewish community.

Perhaps it was only the Irish Catholic, New England upbringing, but my experience of religion included a lot of commandments and sins, heaven and hell, and the fire and brimstone forecast. Since Jesus was Jewish, I falsely assumed that Judaism and Catholicism would be very similar. This ceremony was warm, inviting, and even somewhat casual. The men in the temple greeted each other with heartfelt hugs and even, in some cases, kisses on the cheek. This was not the more common firm handshake I learned from Father Connerton during my altar boy training at St. Augustine's Church.

What was amazing about this sacrament was that everyone there was focused on celebrating the teenager. All their speeches and toasts at the after-party were about building him up, demonstrating just how much he was loved by so many people, and encouraging him on his journey into adulthood.

I wasted so much time in my teenage years worrying about making mistakes on the basketball court or on the pitcher's mound that I often found myself playing "not to lose" instead of

WHAT KIND OF ART DO GIRAFFES PAINT?

GIRAFFITI.

confidently playing to win. I was so fearful of rejection that I didn't ask a girl to a dance until I was well into my twenties, and I needed liquid courage to do so. If I had this sort of encouragement as a teen, I can't help but wonder how much more enjoyable my childhood might have been and what that might have led me to try much earlier in my life.

I found the ceremony to be the most inspiring religious event of my life and exactly what people that age need. Mazel tov!

I see two other periods in our lives when we need similar reassurance, support, and guidance. Working backward, retirement comes to mind. I just saw my mother retire after sixty years as the hardest-working person I've ever met. Instead of a memorial where we talk about how wonderful someone was after they have passed, I propose we create the "Premorial" to be a gathering of our closest friends and family to boost our spirits and to encourage us as we turn sixty-five, seventy, or seventy-five. This is something I would gladly help someone build into its own industry, hopefully long before I need such encouragement. Who's in?

The other time when we need extra help is when we transition into a new career or business. This could be when we leave the house to get a job, join the military, graduate from college, get kicked out of our parent's house after moving back home after college, or leave a job to start our own venture.

Realizing the importance of having encouraging guides, visionaries, and sentries in your own life is a perfect start to thinking differently. But if you want to truly be the giraffe, you must be this for others as well. That's a posture and default practice you adopt.

You can teach others to avoid masses and asses, to swim upstream, to avoid hyenas and lions, and to be nomads. You can encourage them to lead with their heart instead of their heads, speak, feed, and see everything differently. You can let those who are discouraged know that they will survive the drop to wobble, get their feet under them, and start moving. You will lead by example when you strut your strange stuff and try new things.

One day, while we were sitting at the dinner table, Heather told the kids that I would be going to Chicago the next day. All three of my kids asked interesting questions:

> Kierstin (13): Why are you going to Chicago?
> Dad: I am giving a speech to a group of successful financial advisors.
> Tyler (16): How much do they pay you to do that?
> Dad: $20,000 plus expenses.
> Chloe (10): Wait! What? Who pays *you* to talk?

I used to joke that, with teens and tweens in the house, I go on the road to speak so that someone will listen to what I have to say. The truth is I'm proud to say these giraffe lessons have been noticed and adopted by all three of my kids.

- Tyler joined the Jewish fraternity Alpha Epsilon Pi, and we aren't Jewish.
- Kierstin gave up dance for girl's wrestling, then won her district and region within three years.
- Chloe is passing up on traditional college to follow her passion at art school—possibly abroad.

I was certainly not the perfect father, but I love that all three of my wonderful kids strut their strange stuff with confidence and pride.

You can and should help breed the next generation of giraffes. They are the future of all innovation and the hope for all diversity and inclusion. Nobody's great at it when they start, but we all need to try it.

FOR BUSINESS

At this point in the book, you can see how the giraffe is very different from other animals. The differences start with childbirth and continue with the daily activities of eating, sleeping, and walking. Why does it surprise you that these unusual animals have unique mating rituals? If you live differently, it makes sense that you would be made differently too.

The making of a giraffe starts with tasting the pee and continues through a very long gestation period where the baby giraffe grows inside the mother. After the childbirth drop, normally solitary giraffes will stay in groups to protect the young—and the old, the sick, or the injured. There is a family structure of sorts, and they look out for each other. This is the tower we learned about earlier.

In our wild dog-eat-dog business ecosystem, we must do the same and care for upstart innovators. Being an entrepreneur isn't the easy way. Being an entrepreneur isn't the better way. For anyone who does it, it is the only way. I joke in seminars that I went to business school at UCLA and immediately found out I was infinitely unemployable.

Entrepreneurs are baby giraffes who need guidance, care, and protection from other entrepreneurs. In my experience, successful or seasoned founders are more than willing to help younger proteges. In this chapter, I call upon the giraffes who are reading this to find ways to encourage, embrace, and enjoy the energy of younger entrepreneurs.

This is my cause and what I'm doing now. I want to help inspire and teach future giraffes who would otherwise be unhappy and out of place in a herd. I have a soft spot in my heart for helping those who help others.

Since we, as giraffes, are unique, we must consider both the importance of helping other giraffes find their true calling and the truth that we must employ new, unique, and potentially off-putting

TODAY'S REACH

methods of doing so. Giraffes don't want to fit in so, ironically, we sometimes need to be persistent and patient, even when trying to help them! Try anyway.

If you don't think you have anything to offer, you're probably an ideal person to help. For this reason, I only have one challenge for you:

What's one thing you should try to expand your horizons and connect with a tower? As always, I encourage you not to overthink this. If you're stuck, ask another giraffe. There are opportunities all around you. Maybe someone's invited you to try Spenga®. (Okay, bad example.) Stop, look around, pick one, and take the scary step. Hold your nose if necessary.

CHAPTER 14

DON'T FALL ASLEEP

WHAT SEEMINGLY UNHEALTHY GIRAFFE HABIT CAN SAVE YOUR LIFE AND YOUR BUSINESS?

Giraffes don't sleep. At least not as we'd define it or expect. When humans sleep only an hour or two, it's usually because of an emergency, a regrettable decision at last call, or an unrealistic assumption about our ability to sleep on a red-eye. For a giraffe, the natural sleep cycle is between 30 and 120 minutes per night. Compare that to my teenagers who appear to have the mathematically impossible ability to sleep 120 minutes per *hour*.

Throughout this book, we have explored the vulnerabilities of the giraffe and seen how the giraffe has evolved to leverage these threats into unique strengths. Sleep is yet another example. Because of their large size, a giraffe found sleeping lying down would be both an easy kill and a huge feast for a pride of lions or a clan of hyenas. Huge reward and low risk is the opposite of how you want to be seen on the savanna.

There are three unique factors to a giraffe's sleep routine. First, the giraffe sleeps standing up. This allows the animal to move quickly if it is startled. Second, the giraffe sleeps with its eyes half-open and its ears twitching. The clever animal is never thoroughly checked out, so it is much harder to sneak up on it. Third, you already learned that a giraffe sleeps very little, but it gets even crazier. The giraffe sleeps for five to thirty-five minutes at a time.

Before we dive into what this means for the giraffe, it may make sense to explore *why* this is possible. It's obviously not a specific quantity of sleep the giraffes are seeking. Our long-necked guides have taught us that the quality of the time we spend doing something is what really matters. These short bursts of extremely meditative sleep appear to be enough to keep the giraffe going.

What do all these waking hours mean for the giraffe? You know that giraffes eat standing up, with their eyes fourteen to eighteen feet above the ground. In addition to having a fantastic perspective, the giraffe "stands watch" for so much more time than other animals. An average lion sleeps thirteen to twenty hours per day. Zebras sleep standing up for seven hours. The added time to survey the situation on the plains, plus the better perspective, gives the giraffe a far more accurate awareness of its surroundings than another animal could possibly have.

What does this awareness do for the giraffe? It keeps its ass alive, that's what. While most of the predators are sleeping away the day, the giraffe is awake and moving. While lions and hyenas are dreaming of coming across a giant giraffe, that giraffe is strolling through their territory on its way to safer havens. *Sweet dreams, Simba.*

FOR YOU

Giraffes do "giraffe things" nearly every hour of the day. Our takeaway isn't to sleep less. From firsthand experience, I can assure you that is a horrible long-term plan that will come back to bite you harder than a lion. The lesson we need to take is:

Don't fall asleep in the pursuit of being a giraffe.

For most of my life, I didn't have a problem going all-in on something. Sure, I have written a lot of books, set some sales records at different companies, built and sold companies, and rebounded from nasty litigation more than once, I'm afraid.

When I survey people at conferences, most say, unsurprisingly, that health, family, or spirituality are the most important things in life. Yet, when we track their hours and dollars spent, we find that finances and career are the clear winners. I know that I have treated my body like a temple—unfortunately, like a temple in a holy war.

No fewer than three times, I've made my health a priority and lost more than twenty pounds. This is not part of some impressive biohacking, anti-aging, or biggest loser story. This is more of the yo-yo effect, where I fall back into a pattern of sacrificing my health when I have something "more important," profitable, or supposedly life-changing as my focus.

Lifting your head out of the weeds, surveying the landscape, and finding a different path is not a one-time thing. If you keep an eye on the horizon more regularly, you will find small changes in course to be much less disruptive and far less stressful. Once I set out on this giraffe journey (seemingly alone), I realized I wasn't alone at all. So many people were doing the same thing. When I started to be the giraffe, poof! Other giraffes mysteriously appeared.

In the spring of 2019, I was asked to deliver the keynote address to Penn Mutual Insurance Company's Top Advisor Conference. My dear friend, Mike Dunne, instructed everyone to complete the personal scorecard in their packet. This was a precursor to the Wild Factor assessment you completed. When I asked everyone to share the lowest-scoring area, what I saw was staggering.

Career (3 hands)
Finance (4 hands)
Relationships (1 hand)
Fun (2 hands)
Health (>290 hands)

Ninety-five percent of people said health was their lowest score. This assessment is designed to help people figure out what areas of life are most commonly sacrificed. An overwhelming majority of these successful salespeople reported that their health was the area of life where they were making the most sacrifices.[39]

I have given this assessment to thousands of people. I expected health to be one of the lower scores, but I didn't expect it to represent over 90 percent of my audience of successful people. Caught off guard, I said, "So, you're saying that this job is fucking killing you!"

When I peered through the bright lights, I could see the faces of people in the first few rows. That was a bad decision on my part. I followed up by saying, "Don't shoot the messenger. You filled out those forms before I even took the stage. You knew your health was a problem before I said my first words today."

They knew it, but they really weren't aware in a way that fueled action.

I suggested that attendees focus on being giraffes at this conference for a change. My charge was that they go into every session and workshop looking for strategies, techniques, and strategic partnerships that would help them improve their lowest two scores. The next day, a seventy-year-old industry veteran introduced himself and told me that my presentation was unlike any of the hundreds he had attended in his career. When I asked him how, he responded, "Everyone is quick to offer me content for my decision-making. You are the first person to offer me context." Mission accomplished, Mr. Giraffe.

The lesson from the giraffe being awake twenty-three hours per day is that mindfulness makes all the difference. If we want to improve our health, finances, career, relationships, or fun, we must always keep in mind what we are trying to improve and look for ways to be the giraffe.

When faced with choices and opportunities, we need to be aware of what we are trying to improve in ourselves before we make any decision. Will saying yes help me achieve my goals?

The more aware you are, the more often you will remind yourself, and the more often you will review your goals and affirmations, and the more likely you will make decisions that will help you achieve your goals faster and more easily.

HAVE YOU HEARD THE JOKE ABOUT A GIRAFFE'S NECK?

IT'S A LONG ONE.

That's why I have a fun surprise for you at the back of this book. Don't peek yet.

FOR BUSINESS

Giraffes avoid most potential threats by seeing them long before they appear. Conversely, herd animals have no idea there is a lion ambush until it is happening. Lions rely on chaos and confusion from a surprise attack, as it causes their prey to act abruptly and make mistakes.

I wrote this chapter on a plane to Charlotte, North Carolina. As I put this book aside and read the surveys the employees and owner took for me, I noticed something troubling. Every one of the respondents said that less than 30 percent of their work was pre-planned. Most reported that 80–90 percent of their days were hijacked to fix some important issue. The CEO was unhappy with the production of the team, and the team was frustrated with the CEO's seemingly unending need for them to change course and deal with the fire drill du jour.

When asked, the employees said they could get much more work done if they had one uninterrupted hour each day. When pressed, the CEO conceded that there was never a life-threatening emergency that had to be resolved before noon. The solution was to eliminate the herd mentality and focus on the big picture.

The company implemented "quiet hours" from 8:00 a.m. to noon, Tuesday through Thursday. During those twelve hours each week, you could NOT knock on someone's door, schedule a meeting or a call, send an email or text, or interrupt anyone on the team in any way. During that time, you were expected to complete everything that had been added to your to-do list at the beginning of the week. Since the team asked for five hours each week, and they received twelve, including groups of four hours at a time, as longer blocks of time are needed for more complicated proposals, they were delighted.

The CEO was skeptical but eventually went along with it. I encouraged him to schedule his networking meetings, personal appointments, and weekly golf game during quiet hours so he would be less inclined to break his end of the deal. How did it work out? Within a year of our meeting, the CEO decided to take a call from a business broker. With production up, he received multiple offers to buy his company. All were north of $10 million. His sale closed in 2022, and everyone was happy, especially the once-reluctant giraffe.

If your business is constantly in a rush or panic mode, or you are routinely disrupted from your daily tasks, it's because you are stuck in the weeds. You are so busy "working" that you can't possibly see what is coming your way. Even worse, you don't have time to brainstorm a more efficient process, design a better product or service, or build a better team to implement it.

The giraffe teaches us that businesses should be constantly evolving and always looking for a

THE BEST PART OF BEING SO TALL IN SCHOOL?

YOU CAN PEEK AT YOUR NEIGHBOR'S NOTES!

better path. When you have your eyes on the horizon, you'll identify problems long before they are upon you; there's little chance for a competitor or industry change to sneak up on you and send you into chaos because you are never really asleep.

THE NEXT STEP IN YOUR EVOLUTION—
TO BE THE GIRAFFE

Being the giraffe is not a transaction but rather a transformation. The giraffe teaches us to be aware of who we are, what we need, and why we are doing things. This is so we don't get stuck in the weeds, stumble into the lion's den, or otherwise get lost on our journey.

Congratulations! Completing this book is a great accomplishment, especially considering how much you already have going on in your life. But you don't become a giraffe by reading a book, watching a TEDx Talk, or attending a conference.

To help you along the way, there are several resources to reinforce these lessons.

Check out the Money Differently, Business Differently, and Life Differently bundles if you want to dive deeper into any or all of these areas.

Connect with me on LinkedIn for updates: https://www.linkedin.com/in/chrisjarvis/

Most importantly, check out Giraffe University and
Jarvis Tower offers to work directly with Chris Jarvis.

Like all evolutionary changes, this may not feel natural at first and can take some time. The good news is that each of these steps is habit-forming.

The more often you think about what you're doing, the easier it will be to see what's going on and to imagine what else could be happening in your life and in your business.

See differently   *Business differently*

Money differently   *Life differently!*

Over the last thirty years, I have learned so much from many remarkable teachers—both voluntary and involuntary. At times, I wasn't sure if I was being hanged, but I can see now that I was just lengthening my neck for this journey.

Be the Giraffe is the most important book I've ever written, and I'm grateful you took this much time to share it with me. I hope I can continue to help you and your company in some way in the future. Feel free to email me at: mail@chrisjarvis.me.

Elevate Your Perspective
See a Better Path
Be the Giraffe,

ACKNOWLEDGEMENTS

I'd like to thank Jack Canfield for insisting I NOT co-author a book with him and instead focus on *Be the Giraffe*. This changed my life in ways I couldn't imagine. You were right, brother!

I want to thank my wife Heather for listening to countless neck-stretching ideas and always encouraging me to break free from any and every herd that wants me to join.

To my dear mother Dot Fogarty, your endless love and support are the foundation that allow me to stick my neck out and build bigger and better ways to help others.

Chloe, Kierstin, and Tyler—you are the inspiration for me to take risks and accomplish things that will make you not only admit that I'm your father, but also make you proud to tell people.

Ramon Peralta of Peralta Design, you had a hand in the creation of "the giraffe," and I'll forever be grateful.

Doug Hostetler, Tony Assadi, Bob Chesner, Dan Stanley, and Ron Rimkus—you pushed me to do what really lights me up and made it possible for me to take time away from clients to make it a reality.

Mariah Swift, Brittney Bossnow, and Esther Fedorkevich of The Fedd Agency, you were invaluable in the vision and execution of *Be the Giraffe* as a book, a brand, and a movement.

Last but not least, I can't thank Mike Loomis enough. After years of hashing out many ideas and fine-tuning the wording—this book is a success.

ENDNOTES

1   "Invasive Species," The National Wildlife Federation, accessed October 29, 2023, https://www.nwf.org/Educational-Resources/Wildlife-Guide/Threats-to-Wildlife/Invasive-Species

2   "Invasive and Exotic Marine Species," NOAA Fisheries, accessed September 24, 2023, https://www.fisheries.noaa.gov/insight/invasive-and-exotic-marine-species

3   Chris Jarvis, "Surviving Ain't Thriving—Break Free from the Herd," TEDx Talks, March 25, 2022, 12:36, https://www.youtube.com/watch?v=-8DkqpUK_DQ

4   Dumb and Dumber, directed by Peter Farrelly and Bobby Farrelly (Los Angeles, CA: New Line Cinema, 1994).

5   Dan Sullivan, Our Strategic Coach, accessed September 24, 2023, https://www.strategiccoach.com/our-team/#/people/dan-sullivan-coach/

6   The Cambridge Dictionary, s.v. "balance," accessed October 29, 2023, https://dictionary.cambridge.org/dictionary/learner-english/balance

7   Olivia Guy-Evans, "Pareto Principle (The 80-20 Rule): Examples & More," Simply Psychology, September 21, 2023, https://www.simplypsychology.org/pareto-principle.html

8   Warren Buffett, "Afternoon Session—1996 Meeting Transcript and Video," CNBC, Warren Buffet Archive, https://buffett.cnbc.com/video/1996/05/06/afternoon-session---1996-berkshire-hathaway-annual-meeting.html

9   Austin Carr, "How Steve Jobs's Early Vision for Apple Inspired a Decade of Innovation," Fast Company, October 5, 2011, https://www.fastcompany.com/1776369/video-how-steve-jobss-early-vision-apple-inspired-decade-innovation

10   Alyson Shontel, "The Greatest Comeback Story of All Time: How Apple Went from Near Bankruptcy to Billions in 13 Years," *Business Insider*, October 26, 2010, https://www.businessinsider.com/apple-comeback-story-2010-10#1998-introducing-the-imac-2

11   W. Chan Kim and Renée Mauborgne, Blue Ocean Strategy, (Brighton, MA: Harvard Business Review Press, 2005).

12   Overseas Delivery Tourist, Volvo, accessed September 24, 2023, https://www.volvocars.com/us/l/osd-tourist/

13   The Giraffe Conservation Foundation, "What Are the Main Threats to Giraffe?" accessed October 29, 2023, https://giraffeconservation.org/facts/what-are-the-main-threats-to-giraffe-why-are-their-numbers-declining/

14   *The Oxford Learner's Dictionary*, s.v. "predator," accessed September 24, 2023, https://www.oxfordlearnersdictionaries.com/us/definition/english/predator

15   *The Merriam-Webster Dictionary, s.v. "pride,"* accessed September 24, 2023, https://www.merriam-webster.com/dictionary/pride

16   *The Merriam-Webster Dictionary* Online, s.v. "tower," accessed September 24, 2023, https://www.merriam-webster.com/dictionary/tower

17   Maia Szalavitz, "Touching Empathy," *Psychology Today*, March 1, 2010, https://www.psychologytoday.com/us/blog/born-love/201003/touching-empathy

18   Aimee Groth, "You're the Average of the Five People You Spend the Most Time With," *Business Insider*, July 24, 2012, https://www.businessinsider.com/jim-rohn-youre-the-average-of-the-five-people-you-spend-the-most-time-with-2012-7

19   Allison Sadlier, "1 in 4 Americans Feel They Have No One to Confine in," *New York Post*, April 30, 2019, https://nypost.com/2019/04/30/1-in-4-americans-feel-they-have-no-one-to-confide-in/

20   ABTA The Travel Associate, "24 Interesting Facts About the Kalahari Desert," Signature Safaris, accessed October 29, 2023, https://www.signatureafricansafaris.com/24-interesting-facts-kalahari/; Nina Kokotas Hahn, "The Guide to Africa's Ultimate Migration," September 14, 2020, www.abercrombiekent.com/blog/inspiration/the-ultimate-guide-to-africas-great-migration./

21   Dean Talbot, "Chicken Soup for the Soul Book Series Statistics," Words Rated, July 26, 2023, https://wordsrated.com/chicken-soup-for-the-soul-book-series-statistics/

22　The National Wildlife Federation, "Toads," https://www.nwf.org/Educational-Resources/Wildlife-Guide/Amphibians/Toads#:~:text=If%20they%27re%20brown%20or,if%20a%20predator%20is%20nearby

23　Howard Schultz, Onward, (New York: Rodale Books, 2011).

24　Consultant for Demand Lighting, in discussion with author, 2019.

25　Susan Wojcicki, "On Making Big Decisions," speech, UCLA Anderson School of Management, May 5, 2023, video of speech, https://youtu.be/y2gMTHz6N5o)

26　Alzheimer's Association, https://www.alz.org/

27　Simon Sinek, "Start with Why—How Great Leaders Inspire Action," TEDx Talks, September 8, 2009, 18:01, https://www.youtube.com/watch?v=u4ZoJKF_VuA

28　Adele Peters, "People Are More Likely to Trust -- and Buy -- Purpose-Driven Brands," Fast Company, February 17, 2021, https://www.fastcompany.com/90605135/people-are-more-likely-to-trust-and-buy-purpose-driven-brands?partner=rss&utm_source=rss&utm_medium=feed&utm_campaign=rss+fastcompany&utm_content=rss)

29　Afdhel Aziz, "The Power of Purpose: The Business Case for Purpose (All the Data You Were Looking for, Part 2)," Forbes, March 7, 2020, https://www.forbes.com/sites/afdhelaziz/2020/03/07/the-power-of-purpose-the-business-case-for-purpose-all-the-data-you-were-looking-for-pt-2/?sh=5e85bf803cf7

30　Shane McFeely and Ben Wigert, "This Fixable Problem Costs U.S. Businesses $1 Trillion," Gallup, March 13, 2019, https://www.gallup.com/workplace/247391/fixable-problem-costs-businesses-trillion.aspx

31　Giulia Carbonaro, "Boomers Dying Out Could Lead to a Colossal Transfer of Wealth," Newsweek, April 26, 2023, https://www.newsweek.com/boomers-millennials-transfer-wealth-future-1795099#:~:text=Millennials%20are%20expected%20to%20hold,it%20overall%2C%20experts%20told%20Newsweek.

32　Erin Casey, "Zig Ziglar's Lessons From the Top," Success, August 26, 2008, https://www.success.com/zig-ziglars-lessons-from-the-top/

33　The San Diego Zoo, "Giraffe," accessed October 29, 2023, https://animals.sandiegozoo.org/animals/giraffe

34   Nigel Holloway, "How USAA Drives the Highest Customer Loyalty in the Insurance Industry," *Forbes*, December 2, 2020, https://www.forbes.com/sites/salesforce/2020/12/02/how-usaa-drives-the-highest-customer-loyalty-in-the-insurance-industry/?sh=45f3b9b03b71

35   Giraffe Conservation Fund, "Giraffe Facts: Starting Life,," accessed October 29, 2023, https://giraffeconservation.org/facts/starting-life/

36   Arnold. Netflix. 2023. https://www.netflix.com/title/81317673

37   Heb. 11:1-2

38   Michael Gartenberg, "Now Apple's Really 'for the Rest of Us,'" Macworld, June 22, 2010, https://www.macworld.com/article/206163/gartenberg_restofus.html; E*TRADE, "Sugar Momma," AdForum, accessed October 29, 2023, https://www.adforum.com/creative-work/ad/player/6062/sugar-momma/etrade

39   Chris Jarvis, "See Differently, Business Differently: Giraffe Tips from a Million Dollar Producer" presentation, Focus 2019 Adviser Forum by Penn Mutual, June 2019.

"You're not too big. This room is too small!"

FREE BONUS

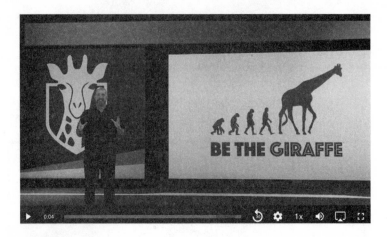

I wrote *Be the Giraffe* to elevate perspectives and reveal paths to different outcomes.

To help you Money Differently, Business Differently, and Life Differently, I have included additional resources absolutely free!

Here is what you will receive:

- Video training, explaining how to get the most out of *Be the Giraffe*
- Exercises and worksheets
- Assessment tools for you, your family, your colleagues, and your employees
- E-newsletter subscription
- Useful links
- And much more!

You get everything at www.chrisjarvis.me/btg/bonus or by scanning the QR Code below

www.chrisjarvis.me/btg/bonus

FIND YOUR
WILD Factor

Are you ready to get more out of your career,
improve your finances, live healthier, build
stronger relationships and have more fun?

FIND OUT HOW YOUR INNER
ANIMAL CAN GUIDE YOU

Take the Find Your Wild Factor assessment for FREE
Use code 17CJ44 and you and save $19.99

GO WILD

https://chrisjarvis.me/wildfactor-exam/

 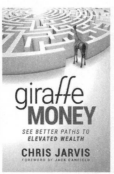  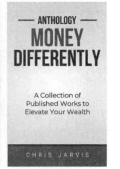

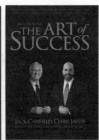

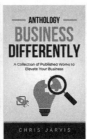

life
DIFFERENTLY

YOU DON'T HAVE TO SACRIFICE YOUR HEALTH OR YOUR HAPPINESS TO BE RICH OR SUCCESSFUL!

The Life Differently Bundle will teach you how to improve your finances, get more out of your career, build deeper relationships, live healthier, and have more fun along the way.

Life Differently bundle includes the UNCAGED virtual course, with over 50 videos, worksheets, and exercises. (regularly $499)

Order today and receive
all this for only $97

www.chrisjarvis.me/lifedifferently

ARE YOU READY TO ELEVATE YOUR BUSINESS AND YOUR LIFE?

GiraffeU is the only group mentoring program that will help you money differently, business differently, and life differently!

- Live weekly trainings with Chris Jarvis
- Focused on money, business and life improvement
- Small group (<25 people) learning environment
- Meet experts in various fields
- Connect with like-minded business owners
- Advanced financial solutions at deep discounts
- Access to proprietary materials
- Tickets to live events
- And so much more!

To learn how to make more money, build a more valuable and impactful business, and get more out your life, apply to be part of the next cohort at Giraffe University today.

www.giraffeu.com

JARVIS**TOWER**

WORK 1-ON-1 WITH CHRIS JARVIS

- Save millions of dollars in income tax – legally!
- Learn how to "Be your own bank" and fund future growth
- Eliminate unnecessary taxes on investment gains
- Avoid pitfalls and maximize the value of your company at sale
- Create a $0 estate tax liability without giving it away
- Protect family wealth from divorce without using a prenup
- Structure family wealth in ways that support your values
- Avoid excess fees from CPAs, attorneys and financial advisors
- Learn to enjoy the success you have created for yourself

If your business has over $50M in revenue or over $5M in annual profit, or your net worth is between $25M and $250M, you are likely missing out on invaluable wealth secrets used by billionaires and savvy corporations.

Apply today to see how joining the Tower will help you see things differently.

APPLY NOW

www.chrisjarvis.me/application